SMART TEACHING

Using Brain Research and Data to Continuously Improve Learning

SMART TEACHING

Using Brain Research and Data to Continuously Improve Learning

Ronald Fitzgerald, D.Ed.

ASQ Quality Press
Milwaukee, Wisconsin

American Society for Quality, Quality Press, Milwaukee 53203

© 2006 by American Society for Quality

All rights reserved. Published 2005

Printed in the United States of America

12 11 10 09 08 07 06   5 4 3 2 1

Library of Congress Cataloging-in-Publication Data

Fitzgerald, Ronald, 1933–

    Smart teaching : using brain research and data to continuously improve
learning / Ronald Fitzgerald.

      p. cm.

    Includes index.

    ISBN 0-87389-661-0 (alk. paper)

    1. Effective teaching.   2. Learning, Psychology of.   3. Brain.   I. Title.

LB1025.3.F58 2005

371.102—dc22

                                       2005014719

Publisher: William A. Tony

Acquisitions Editor: Annemieke Hytinen

Project Editor: Paul O'Mara

Production Administrator: Randall Benson

ASQ Mission: The American Society for Quality advances individual, organizational, and
community excellence worldwide through learning, quality improvement, and knowledge
exchange.

Attention Bookstores, Wholesalers, Schools, and Corporations: ASQ Quality Press books, videotapes,
audiotapes, and software are available at quantity discounts with bulk purchases for business,
educational, or instructional use. For information, please contact ASQ Quality Press at 800-248-1946,
or write to ASQ Quality Press, P.O. Box 3005, Milwaukee, WI 53201-3005.

To place orders or to request a free copy of the ASQ Quality Press Publications Catalog, including
ASQ membership information, call 800-248-1946. Visit our Web site at www.asq.org or
http://qualitypress.asq.org.

Quality Press
600 N. Plankinton Avenue
Milwaukee, Wisconsin 53203
Call toll free 800-248-1946
Fax 414-272-1734
www.asq.org
http://qualitypress.asq.org
http://standardsgroup.asq.org
E-mail: authors@asq.org

♾ Printed on acid-free paper

Contents

List of Figures

Acknowledgments

This guide was produced on the basis of work by many dedicated people associated with Minuteman Regional High School in Lexington, Massachusetts. The Minuteman School Committee members, with their support of staff training and resources, made our efforts to develop an effective system possible. With their daily use of the principles and concepts in the system, dozens of Minuteman teachers and hundreds of students have verified the power of managing learning with data to achieve continuous improvement in student achievement. With their special encouragement, my wife Sylvia and the spouses of many teachers and administrators gave us the energy to experiment with system improvements. Special contributions to the system and the guide were made by Sebastian Paquette, a teacher who has implemented the system in ways that have encouraged the highest levels of student motivation and achievement. With wonderful patience and talent, Janice Smith processed the pages and figures for the guide. The production illustrates a fundamental component in a good teaching system—teamwork.

—Ron Fitzgerald
Former Teacher and
Superintendent

CD-ROM Instructions

The following files* are available on the accompanying CD-ROM for this book. The numbering of the figures corresponds exactly to that in the book. To access these files, you will need Adobe Acrobat Reader 5.0 or higher and/or Microsoft PowerPoint.

Read Me file

file name: **ReadMe.pdf**

Introduction figure and Figures 1 through 26

file names: **Figures1-26.pdf**
               Figures1-26.ppt

Figures 27 through 48

file names: **Figures27-48.pdf**
               Figures27-48.ppt

Tables, guides, and checklists

file name: **TablesGuidesChecklists.pdf**

The color graphics can greatly enhance presentations to staff groups and/or in-service training sessions. Be sure to relate each to the appropriate information provided in the workshop-in-a-handbook publication for maximum impact. Of course, you should add interactive exercise and/or follow-up activities to each major point covered. The resource is intended to promote application, not theoretical discussion. For additional relevant materials, see the author's web page at www.SmartTeaching.org.

---

* These files are intended for the reader's personal use only. The purchaser of the handbook may use the files for personal presentations and school projects. They should not be reproduced for any other use without the prior written permission of the publisher. All such requests should be directed to ASQ Quality Press at 800-248-1946 or qpress@asq.org.

Sample Results of Using a System* Approach to Teaching

1. Percent passing state language arts test on *first* try in grade 10:

   Year 1 = 55%

   Year 2 = 83%

   Year 3 = 86%

   Year 4 = 91%

   … while enrollment of disadvantaged learners increased from 36% to 53%

2. Average annual grade equivalent gain in reading skill, grade 9 lab:

   Year 1 = 2.28 grade levels   Year 3 = 2.81 grade levels

   Year 2 = 2.53 grade levels   Year 4 = 3.44 grade levels

3. Improvement in classroom project scores in an English class:

   Year 1 = median 73.0, standard deviation 12.0

   Year 2 = median 82.0, standard deviation 8.4

   Year 3 = median 90.0, standard deviation 6.3

*The SMART TEACHING system

An Introduction to Using This Book

This section is provided to help you use the book effectively. One immediate clarification is that you are hereby granted permission under the copyright to copy graphics, guides, checklists, and forms for local instructional purposes. As you plan the use of materials, consider the following major points about the book.

The Unique Format

Throughout most of the book, pages are presented in sets—explanatory text on the right-hand page and figure or other related information on the left-hand page. For example, the Introduction figure shows three sample results of using a system approach to teaching. Each sample will be discussed more fully later in the book. For now, the example simply emphasizes that the system works and familiarizes you with the format. This format is used in order to:

1. Allow individuals to study topical page sets where the text is reinforced with visual presentations.
2. Allow staff developers and teacher trainers to copy graphics and guides as either transparencies or handouts for seminars or classes. *Note*: A CD-ROM containing the figures as PowerPoint and PDF color transparencies and guides is provided at the end of the book.
3. Provide the option of turning the book sideways and quickly flipping through the figures pages to either preview or review major points covered.

The format is designed as a workshop tool to support each of these study options.

Emphasis on System

The book promotes a system, or SMART TEACHING, approach to improving student achievement. W. Edwards Deming helped many organizations achieve world-class quality by emphasizing four major principles for continuous improvement:

1. *The need to define and continuously refine a system for pursuing quality.* This book defines a SMART TEACHING system for world-class teaching and learning. You can use the book to establish the system in your classroom or school.
2. *The need to use a model of knowledge to guide your system efforts.* This guide presents the contemporary model of brain-compatible teaching to support continuous improvement in teaching and learning.

3. *The need to base improvement efforts on sensitivity to human psychology.* This guide emphasizes some of the human realities that should not be ignored in classrooms and schools. Unfortunately, some of those realities were not properly recognized in the initial implementation of the No Child Left Behind Act. You can use this guide to seek corrections in flawed processes.

4. *The need to use data to manage improvement efforts* as opposed to using humans to achieve absolute scores. You can use this guide to evaluate your practices.

No one component of the system should be neglected. It takes all parts or components to achieve maximum positive impact. Educators or trainers who focus primarily on one factor, such as learning styles, are not going to achieve the best possible results.

Emphasis on Practical Application

The book is designed for practitioners in grades K–12 or even adult classes. It spends no time taking sides on ivory tower debates that occur, for example, on whether a certain characteristic of a learner is a "talent" or an "intelligence." If a student has a strong ability to think or to produce products or knowledge with his or her visual skills, we want to recognize and use that fact rather than engage in a debate on how to classify the origin of that ability.

To avoid some of the confusion about "styles" present among different books, readers are asked to be conscious of the distinction used in this book:

1. A *learning style* is defined as a way of perceiving or receiving information. Consult the glossary to review terms.

2. A *talent* or *intelligence* or *thinking style* is defined as a way of producing information and/or products.

A learner might prefer to receive information in the visual mode or style but might not prefer or even have strong ability to produce information or products through personal visualization or drawing techniques. In other words, he or she could be a visual learner but not yet have strong visual (production) talents. This book suggests that a teacher can use that practical information without worrying about the common debate on whether a talent is a type of intelligence. Our task in the classroom is to promote learning without being sidetracked by debate irrelevant to our purpose.

Broad but Simple Definition of Brain Research

As the final resource section of this book makes clear, the very simple system components are derived from many resources—neuroscience, cognitive research projects, and observation of practice and results in K–12 and adult classrooms. The phrase *brain research* is by no means limited to the neuroscience field, where much research has not yet been translated into direct implications for teaching practice. This book concentrates on proposing a set of very basic techniques that have proven effective in K–12 and adult classrooms. It concentrates on presenting techniques, not the differing theories found in books listed in the resource section. It is a how-to book. The components of the system have been thoroughly tested over 10 years in Minuteman Regional High School in Lexington, Massachusetts, where the author was the superintendent when this book was prepared. The defined components are not detailed prescriptions. They leave details open to individual teacher creativity. However, the components are fundamental to teaching and learning success on all levels because they rest on such basic and well-documented principles and practices as these:

1. Instruction is more effective if well planned to achieve specific purposes.
2. Students learn more if they are motivated first.
3. Different students have different learning styles and talents.
4. Learning is facilitated by providing relevant learning options so that students can make choices relative to their styles and talents.
5. Careful use of data can help students and teachers improve learning.
6. Documented success encourages more success.

For our purposes, brain research is any research that identifies principles and practices that can promote better learning.

Major Themes of the Book

The system presented in this book rests on these four themes:

1. Many basic teaching techniques that encourage improved learning in K–12 and adult classrooms are now well documented.
2. For the most part, these techniques are not difficult to use.
3. There are simple data analysis tools that should be used in the classroom to adjust teaching and to foster continuous improvement in learning.
4. Teachers and administrators are responsible for ensuring comprehensive and systematic use of the basic teaching techniques and the simple but effective data analysis tools.

This book can help any educator grow and expand a system that will make teaching more effective and more fun. Of course, that system should be pursued on a schoolwide and districtwide basis as well as in individual classrooms. That is the positive requirement that is the foundation of the national No Child Left Behind Act. More important, every student and every family has a right to expect such pursuit of quality in every classroom.

Suggestions on Workshops and Classes

Based on the author's experience, the suggestions following are offered:

1. *For workshops in a school or district.* Two separate full-day workshops are suggested. One can cover the basics of brain-compatible techniques. The other can cover the use of data analysis in the classroom, especially *after* teachers are familiar with brain-compatible techniques whose impact can be measured through data collection and analysis. The data workshop is most successful if all participants have access to a computer and to relevant software such as QI Macros, described in the resources portion of the book. Brief (one- or two-hour) workshops are not effective because they cannot include enough interactivity and hands-on practice.
2. *For courses or college classes.* The book can provide a basic reference for a course on a brain-compatible teaching system. Each topic should then be expanded with listed references and with assigned individual and group production tasks. The goal for each student must be to develop measurable skill in using each component of a system. Strong use of the book can move a course into the forefront of contemporary teaching and quality management in the classroom.

SMART TEACHING

Using Brain Research and Data to Continuously Improve Learning

Figure 1

It Takes a System

Motivate — Defense strategies — Offense strategies

Plan — Do — Check/Adjust — Winning in football

Motivate — Style strategies — Talent strategies

Receiving information — Developing meaning and skills — Winning at learning

A. Why Bother Using a Teaching System?

Study the simplified analogy in Figure 1 on the left-hand page. Complex processes, those that involve adjustment of multiple factors, require a system approach for maximum quality to be achieved.

A football team with a consistent weakness in one major component of its system is unlikely to win the Super Bowl championship. A teaching process that has a consistent weakness in a major component of the process is not going to lead to the highest possible degree of student learning.

The message of this book is that educators should use research to construct and implement a teaching system because that can lead to better learning results than could otherwise be achieved. The book presents a tested and successful teaching system.

Motivating students does not guarantee that they will understand. Even when motivated, some students learn differently than others. There is no method of teaching that works for all students. Therefore, an effective teaching system is one that offers different options to different students. This book, then, does not present one way of teaching. Rather, it shows basic process factors that should be addressed with specific learning options.

Before continuing, let us define the term *system*, as it is used repeatedly in this book. A system is a process constructed by:

1. Identifying major factors or actions that promote reaching some outcome that we wish to achieve
2. Arranging those factors or actions in a relationship (not necessarily an exact sequence or process) that we believe will achieve the desired result
3. Regularly measuring our results and changing the factors, actions, and/or sequence in order to continuously improve the quality of our results

Naturally, a collection of research and/or theories provides the model on which we build a system. In this case, our model is contemporary and continuously evolving information on brain-compatible teaching techniques.

Be aware that the terms *brain-based teaching*, *brain-compatible teaching*, *accelerated learning*, and *differentiated teaching* are all very similar. They all refer to the fact that researchers have discovered that certain activities promote learning better than others and that these activities sometimes differ for different students. This book does not recommend any narrow, fixed, or commercial model. Rather, it presents broad principles of system management and broad principles of brain-compatible teaching in a way that will leave any teacher or trainer with maximum freedom to practice the art as well as the science of great teaching. None of the factors or principles are complicated. So, by examining each general factor separately, we can follow a simple and manageable path to the effective use of a combination of powerful factors for promoting learning.

Figure 2

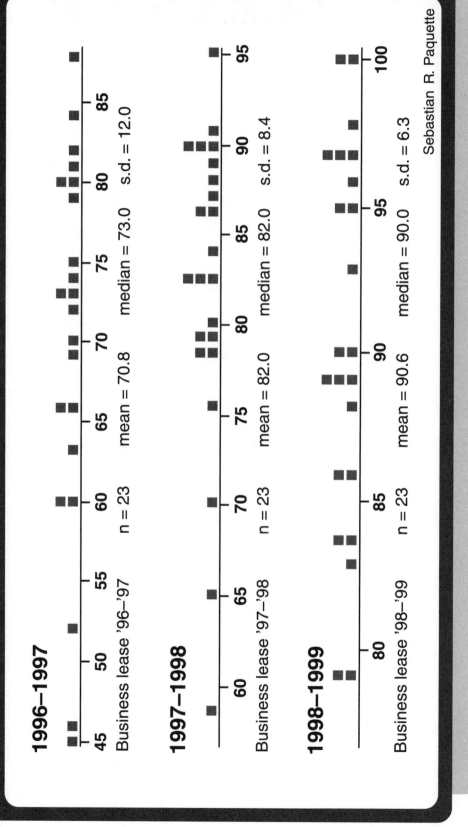

English for the Entrepreneur:
Creating a Business Lease

A major reason for using a system based on the brain-compatible teaching model is that it works so well. Review Figure 2. It summarizes some results from a high-school course that introduced a brain-compatible system in the 1997–98 school year.

The chart shows a distribution of grades in a computer-based unit on creating a business lease. Completion of the unit task was evaluated using a standardized rubric. Consider these realities from the classes of the talented teacher involved:

1. In 1996–97, the class of 23 students was taught with a primary emphasis on traditional techniques:
   - Lecture presentations
   - Reading
   - Assignment of memorization tasks
   - Class review of samples
   - Completion of a production task
2. Beginning in 1997–98, the teacher began using components of a brain-compatible system such as:
   - Pre-assessment of existing knowledge
   - Teaching students about different ways of learning
   - Following a system cycle that started with "anchoring" and a "connecting" or "hooking" experience (more on these later)
   - Giving choices in assignments, such as writing a paragraph or designing a mind map or (for extra credit) both
   - Using real-life examples or stories from the students about their related experiences, always helping students to create colorful images on concepts and information
   - Provoking debates on business and related social issues
   - Open-forum analysis of a sample lease with shared stories on related issues
   - Assigning group tasks (cooperative learning) followed by informal (non-threatening) oral reports
   - Completion of a production task with interspersed reflection
3. A comparison of results between 1996–97 and 1998–99 shows these realities for classes of 23 students in each case:

	1996–97	1998–99
Mean or average grade	70.8	90.6
Standard deviation	12.0	6.3

The standard deviation dropping to 6.3 is an important indicator of quality in this case, because it means less variation from a higher quality average. That reduction in variation from a higher quality point is a classic illustration of measured improvement in results.

Perhaps just as important as higher achievement, both the teacher and the students in this course and other brain-compatible system courses were very enthusiastic about how much more they enjoyed the teaching and learning in the changed classes. The use of planned motivation techniques and variety in interactive learning options generates high levels of engagement and enjoyment. Learning truly becomes more fun. Success generates pride and the expectation of more success.

Figure 3

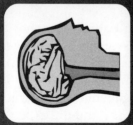

Why Bother with a Teaching System?

1. It takes a system to achieve the best possible results.

2. There is a brain-compatible teaching system that really works.

3. This system is not complicated; YOU can use it.

4. This system makes teaching more effective and even more fun.

The only negative related to these realities is that the students in the brain-compatible system classes often express resentment at some other classes still stuck in more traditional modes. The students become connoisseurs of good teaching. Fortunately, in the case of Minuteman Regional High School in Lexington, Massachusetts, the entire faculty has pursued the implementation of a brain-compatible system. This is an important recommendation for any school or college or company training program—promote a quality system of teaching in *all* classes. Otherwise, students will become discouraged with excessive variation in quality among different classes. "Total quality" is a concept that is as important in education as it is in the world of business.

In later sections of the book, other examples of improvement from Minuteman High School will be presented. Be aware, however, that such improvement is common in K–adult classes around the world. A solid summary of examples is presented in *The Learning Revolution*[1] by Gordon Dryden and Dr. Jeannette Vos.

For now, we can simply summarize the "why" of using this teaching system, as shown in Figure 3. It certainly does take more initial study and planning to establish the system than it does to simply lecture, explain, and assign readings and practice in the traditional manner. However, teachers who make this initial effort become more successful in their mission and enjoy their work more. That increased success and enjoyment is a great reward for using a brain-compatible teaching-learning system.

In the next chapter, an overview of system components is presented. Three cautions are offered in relation to the system:

1. The system is not all-inclusive. New information and improved techniques are being developed regularly, so all educators and trainers should become serious students of research on brain-compatible teaching and learning.

2. Both the components of the system and certainly the sequence of actions should be open to change. That change can be a matter of teacher or trainer preference, student preference, or regular use of the check-and-adjust component of quality management.

3. There are many other factors that contribute to effective teaching and learning, factors not covered in this presentation. The basic message here is, do not skip the basic factor of having a system approach to teaching.

---

1. Gordon Dryden and Dr. Jeannette Vos, *The Learning Revolution* (Torrance, CA: The Learning Web, 1999).

Figure 4

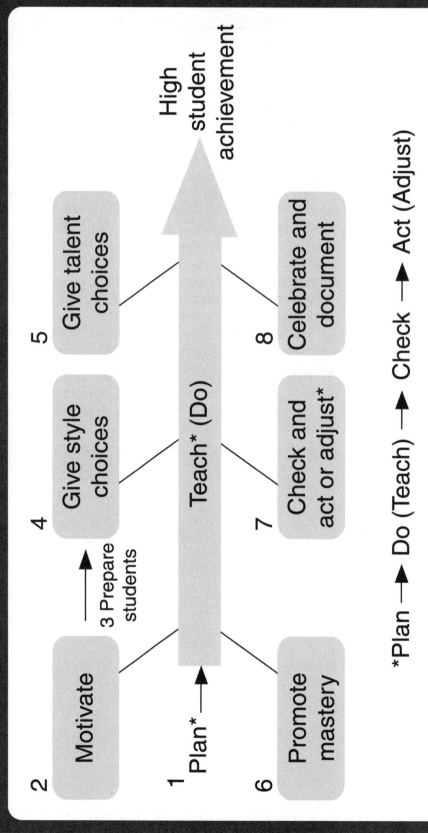

Teaching-Learning System
(The Structure of Section B of the Book)

High student achievement

5 Give talent choices

4 Give style choices

3 Prepare students

2 Motivate

1 Plan*

Teach* (Do)

8 Celebrate and document

7 Check and act or adjust*

6 Promote mastery

*Plan → Do (Teach) → Check → Act (Adjust)

B. What Are the Basic Factors in a System for Quality Teaching?

Figure 4 presents primary factors that greatly influence the effectiveness of teaching and learning. These factors, which are sometimes addressed separately or in a fragmented manner in teacher training programs, are related in a sequence called the Plan → Do → Check → Act/Adjust, or PDCA process, in which *do* stands for *teach*.

Here are some brief comments on each factor:

1. *Plan*. Planning is the fundamental first step in creating any system for achieving results. While this guide is not primarily about planning, Section B-1 does present important points to consider on this factor. Good prior planning is the foundation for good teaching.

2. *Motivate*. Some educators build a plan and then implement their teaching by immediately imparting subject matter to students. This avoids a basic professional responsibility—working first to ensure that all students appreciate the value of what will be covered in a learning unit. Educators who make the mistake of skipping motivation activities are often doomed to the disappointment of working with too many students who are not interested in what is being taught.

3. *Prepare students*. Once motivated, a student can be helped to learn how to learn. This involves assisting each student to learn about himself or herself. A student who knows how he or she learns best is a more effective learner. It is tragic to see a class or school where this help has not been extended to students.

4. *Give style choices*. Some students are comfortable with abstract concepts; others learn best from a concrete or practical context. Given this reality, it is important that the plan for a teaching-learning system gives attention to the value of different individual learning styles.

5. *Give talent choices*. Individual students have different talent strengths. Task options that allow students to capitalize on their talents are a basic way of increasing student involvement and levels of learning.

6. *Promote mastery*. We would not want to be passengers on an airplane where the pilot got 80 percent of the landing procedure correct. Teaching units should be designed to encourage each student to gain full mastery of skills, not to accept 80 percent mastery as "good enough."

7. *Check and act or adjust*. While we need to strive for full mastery with our students, learning systems are complex. Quality, then, should become a continuous journey in which we analyze the effectiveness of our system each time we teach a unit. Then, with our student partners, we should try to identify ways of improving, changing, or adjusting components of the system to reach higher levels of effectiveness in the future.

8. *Celebrate and document*. Success encourages confidence and progress toward more success. Celebrating a student's mastery of learning is an important teaching technique. The record of mastery can serve as important information for the next teacher, who faces the fundamental responsibility of taking each student from where he or she is to new heights of achievement.

Figure 5

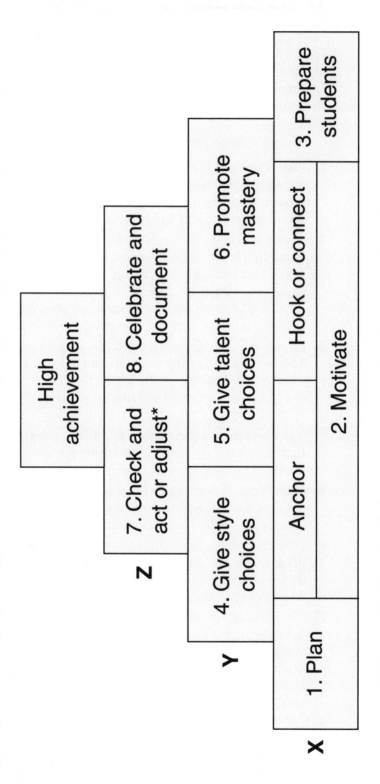

Teaching-Learning System

	High achievement	
7. Check and act or adjust*	8. Celebrate and document	
Z		
4. Give style choices	5. Give talent choices	6. Promote mastery
Y		
Anchor	Hook or connect	3. Prepare students
1. Plan	2. Motivate	
X		

* The word *adjust* is a little more accurate than the general word *act* in teaching.

There are many other factors, components, or techniques that can and should be addressed as we constantly improve the effectiveness of teaching and learning. For example, effective questioning techniques can greatly improve the learning process. The point in this section, however, is that *the eight system factors or components listed here are primary or basic*. Not one of these eight components should be neglected in constructing strong teaching-learning units. Skipping or neglecting any one of the components is a guarantee of lowered effectiveness in the teaching process.

Refer to Figure 5 for another view of the eight primary system factors that constitute a "secret" system for SMART TEACHING. The term *secret* here refers to two basic facts:

1. Too few teacher training programs address the extensive task of giving future teachers the system context for practicing their profession.
2. Critics of the teaching profession often have no knowledge of the research related to each of these components. So, in political processes, they encourage the simplistic, superficial, and erroneous idea that good teaching consists simply of knowing your subject matter and making students work.

The second point must be totally rejected and corrected in order to achieve the best progress in serving students. Knowledge of subject matter is very important. However, knowledge of and the ability to use primary teaching system components is equally important.

The rows of building blocks in Figure 5 provide an insight into applying the system approach to any unit of instruction:

1. Row X = Pre-teaching components, important to setting the stage for the best learning
2. Row Y = Learning components, the heart of the art and science of the teaching process
3. Row Z = Post-teaching components, important to encouraging and arranging future success

This book presents a separate section on each of these components. Do not interpret their numbered order as rigid and inflexible, a point that will be explained in the separate section on each factor. However, there is some strong logic to the general cycle of events. Of course, planning comes first. However, activities under other factors might at times occur in different sequences. This will be explained in the separate factor sections of the book.

Figure 6

Brain-Compatible
Teaching Quality Model

Plan → Then teach:*

Motivate
- Safe
- Possible
- Relevant …
- Anchor
- Hook …

↑

Learning styles
- Auditory
- Visual
- Somatic
- Reflective
- Combinations

↑

Multiple talents
- Eight + (EI)
- Cross impact
- Solve and create
- Use strengths
- Develop strengths

↑

… with real interactivity

Mastery
- Time factors
- Check and act*
- Use data*
- Teaming

↑

Check and adjust*
- Seek reactions*
- Analyze data*
- Define suggestions
- Re-plan

↑

Celebrate
- Performance certification
- Portfolio
- Celebration
- Data summary*

*TQM

Before proceeding to the section on planning, study Figure 6. This figure integrates elements of a brain-compatible teaching model into the primary components of the teaching system. Some of the elements in this model are based on years of observation and cognitive research on what works in classrooms. Some are based on evolving theories and discoveries coming from the rapidly growing field of neuroscience. Magnetic resonance imaging, PET scans, and other new technologies have greatly accelerated the rate of production of new knowledge. Some of that new knowledge has been carefully translated into implications for teaching. Some of the new knowledge is not yet fully understood and can easily be misused, especially by vendors anxious to claim that their products or systems have a basis in science. So the elements of brain-compatible quality teaching used in this system have been carefully selected. They are basic and have been tested in classrooms. Still, it is recommended that all educators become students of brain-compatible research and constantly expand their repertoire of techniques.

Figure 6 is provided here to give you a preview of the fit between brain-compatible techniques and the system presentation in this guide. Some elements are named a little differently than they might be in presentations by others. For example, *multiple talents* is used rather than *multiple intelligences* in order to avoid wasting time on the debate that occurs between those who oppose what they consider to be the theory of multiple intelligences and those who are literal supporters of that concept. Any experienced teacher has learned that some students have more visual or artistic talent than others. Any experienced teacher has learned that some students have more interpersonal skills than others. Section B-5, "Providing Learning Task or Talent Choices," provides proven ways to use such facts and methods that increase the effectiveness of teaching and learning. Put more succinctly, our focus here is on the practical; we leave abstract debate to others and to the impact of continuing research.

Figure 6 repeats the Plan → Do/Teach → Check → Adjust cycle used to introduce this section. That cycle is the basis for continuous improvement in what many business and industry leaders now often label *total quality management*, or TQM. Many schools and districts across the nation use TQM or TQE (total quality education) procedures because continuous improvement is a necessity in a competitive global economy. Section B-8 explains the cycle in more detail. To end these initial comments, however, let us emphasize the word *total*. The continuous improvement process is not something to be pursued in one or a few classrooms. This guide is dedicated to a more practical principle—that the process and system need to be pursued in all (the total) of the classrooms in a school and in all of the schools in a district. For our purposes, quality is a continuous improvement journey and a gift we owe to all students.

Be aware that some other authors emphasize different aspects of quality, such as the use of a numerical rating system (Baldrige, ISO standards, and so on), to evaluate efforts at quality. However, Dr. Deming's principles, which he called "profound knowledge," are simply focused on continuous improvement. He did not use the term *total quality*. He was not a proponent of number-based rating systems. So, in this book, we shall stay focused on defining quality in education as the pursuit of continuous improvement in learning processes and results.

Figure 7

Planning Instruction

Defining measurable target objectives for student performance

1 Customer or student data

2 District and school requirements

3 State/Federal and employer requirements

Gaining information
Organizing a course

4 Deciding what is possible

5 Organizing units and resources

6 Sharing and shaping with students

B-1. The Planning Factor

Planning is necessary to prepare an effective course. This guidebook is *not* about course planning. However, this brief section is included to be sure that you have considered and/or been given what you need to ensure that your course is well planned.

Refer to Figure 7. Be sure you have the answers to these basic questions related to the first three items on the chart:

1. *Student data*: Who are your students? What is their general background or range of backgrounds, including information on previous learning?

2. *District and school requirements*: A district or a school usually has certain learning requirements that a course or group of courses is expected to promote. What are these requirements? Are they realistic in terms of information on previous learning of the students?

3. *State/Federal and employer requirements*: Federal and state accountability laws have led to the promulgation of curriculum frameworks and associated tests across the nation. What are the frameworks and associated assessments that relate to your course or courses? Are they consistent with standards from professional associations like the National Council of Teachers of Mathematics? Do they mesh with standards for preparing for college and Scholastic Aptitude Tests and/or with employer expectations of the development of occupational skills in the case of vocational school students?

Next, you will need to organize your course or courses in relation to the second set of three items:

4. *Deciding what is possible*: Does it appear that students are ready to achieve school, state, and other expectations? If not, what can you or others do about that? What reasonable performance objectives can you establish for the students?

5. *Organizing units and resources*: This guide is focused primarily on helping you with items 5 and 6 in the planning process. What sequences, activities, and techniques can best be organized to help students accomplish the measurable performance objectives defined for a course?

6. *Sharing and shaping with students*: What evaluation and choice partnerships can you define with students to make a course more relevant and attractive to them?

This guide assumes that school or district officials and peers will give you extensive help with the first three or four planning items. However, even if you are handed a previously successful course, you will need to address items 1, 5, and 6 again. Let us look at each.

On gaining student data, data on new students are never the same as data on past students. You need to begin with one of the most important brain realities here: *New information and skills are acquired most effectively when they can be connected to or built on previously acquired information and skills.* Using this reality is a powerful technique that no teacher should ignore. Let us look at some suggestions on this.

Figure 8

Gaining Student Data: The Big Three

1. Pre-survey to discover what information and skills a student already has.

2. Determine a student's special interests and aspirations.

3. Identify a student's learning style and talent preferences.

Review item 1 in Figure 8. It does not use the term *pre-test*. It suggests a *pre-survey*. You are not going to give grades. You are simply determining what information a student already has so that you can build on or connect to that with your teaching. The suggestion is that, after you distribute a unit overview or outline, you use a simple pre-survey to determine the background status of each student. Be sure the students know that it is not a test for grading purposes, but will be used to adjust your instruction to their needs. Later, you can compare the pre-survey results with actual post-test results to evaluate the effectiveness of the instruction.

Consider item 2 in Figure 8. The simple pre-survey for a unit can include questions on special interests at the end, such as:

- Do you have any questions you would like to have answered in this unit?
- What interests you most about the unit?
- What interests you least?
- Is there anything special you would like to do in relation to the topics in the unit?

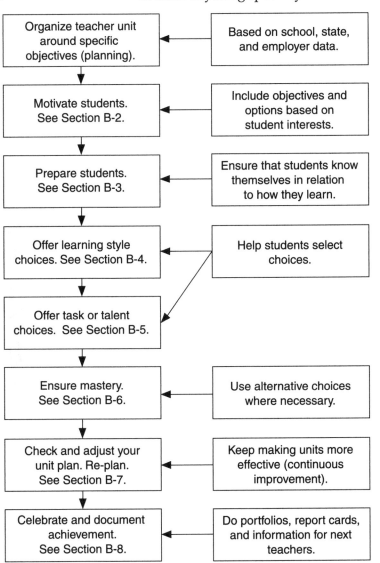

Answers to these questions can help you select or add activity options that will help build student interest in learning.

Finally, item 3 in Figure 8 refers to the value of discovering the learning style and talent preferences of students. Again, this information will help you select motivating learning activities. It is so important that detailed attention is given to the use of a preference test in Section B-3 of this guide.

The information you gather can be used in the ways shown in the flow diagram to the left.

Let us now move to Section B-2 to consider the critical topic of motivating students.

Figure 9

Effects of Emotion

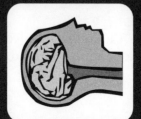

Emotion shifts learning potential in the brain:

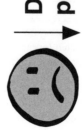

Downshift potential

- Threat
- Boredom
- Tension
- Fear

Upshift

- Safety
- Challenge
- Humor
- Fun

Pre-assess for the flow zone

B-2. Motivation Factors

This section presents a critical concern for educators charged with arranging highly effective teaching and learning. It is a concern often neglected by those who erroneously believe that knowing subject matter is adequate preparation for teaching. The concern is emotions.

The readiness of individual students to profit from teaching is heavily determined by their emotions. This is true because research has shown clearly that brains affected by emotions of fear, pessimism, or boredom are focused on survival or escape; they are not focused on or motivated for learning from their environment.

Figure 9 summarizes this reality and provides us with the basis for a major message. The message is that *good teaching should begin with a specific focus on motivating students by giving attention to the factors that influence their emotions and their resulting state of attention to learning tasks.* Neglecting emotion is an unacceptable action, the antithesis of good teaching. So, the next page of this guide begins the presentation of factors a teacher should address to ensure positive motivation of students. First, however, let us consider the flow zone item in Figure 9.

If material or tasks are presented to a student before he or she is ready, there is a high probability that this will be threatening and discouraging to the student. For example, if a student is expected to deal with algebraic concepts and formulas before mastering basic arithmetic skills, the resulting failure tends to generate fear, anger, or apathy. If a student is expected to solve complex word problems before gaining solid reading skills, the same negative results are likely. The opposite situation—presenting a student with material or tasks already thoroughly mastered—can cause boredom and apathy. This leads to a basic recommendation: *A teacher should always begin a learning unit with a pre-assessment survey or quiz that determines relevant readiness and existing knowledge.* The survey can also ask about special interests or questions the students bring to the unit. Depending on the age of the students, the size of the class or audience, and the records provided by previous teachers, the survey can be oral or written and brief or relatively comprehensive. The important purpose is clear, however: The non-graded survey or quiz allows the teacher to adjust instruction and learning options for individual students. The adjustments should be designed to stay below frustration or non-readiness levels but remain well above the levels of boredom or unnecessary repetition. This appropriate adjustment level is called the *flow* zone, the level at which maximum learning can occur or flow. In some cases, older students might even be referred to different classes or special assistance programs. Remember to seek the flow zone.

Incidentally, the need for learning task adjustment is becoming more and more critical as students and teachers are exposed to an increase in the grade-level specificity and sequential nature of curricula under federal and state curriculum frameworks and assessment legislation. All students do not learn at the same rate. We must teach students, not single grade levels.

Frustration zone: Tasks too difficult
Flow zone: Challenging but possible tasks
Boredom zone: Tasks too easy or repetitious

Figure 10

Factors Contributing to Motivation for Highest Brain Efficiency

1 A safe but challenging environment

2 Confidence in ability to succeed

3 A unique connection experience

4 Presence of useful choices

5 Curriculum perceived as relevant and useful

6 Individualized support and recognition

Anchor

Styles Talents

I can

Real-life tasks

Hook

Teacher-Manager

Highest student motivation

Figure 10 lists some major factors that promote positive emotions and motivation for learning. Here are some related comments:

1. *A safe but challenging environment.* Start your course by *anchoring* your students—saying and doing things that make them feel comfortable with you and with their classmates:

Sample Things to Do	Sample Things to Avoid
Introduce yourself and your interest in helping them gain power through the fun of learning.	Give a lecture on what you will demand from them. (Get them worried early.)
Provide a broad overview of the course and how it can be helpful.	Start with reading and homework assignments in the first session.
Pursue some positive, get-to-know-each-other activities with the class.	Concentrate on subject matter right away.
State and mean that you will help each student learn at his or her own rate and in his or her own way (more on this later). Give examples.	Suggest that each must "keep up" with your schedule and activities for everyone, or else.
Start with two broad rules: 1. Everyone must give respect and courtesy to everyone else. 2. There are no "dumb" questions. Then, have the class help you build the details of these rules.	Explain your many class rules in detail and in relation to punishment or loss of privileges for infractions.

Be sure you continue the context set by this anchoring throughout your course.

2. *Confidence in ability to succeed.* Continue the anchoring process by explaining ways in which you will help if anyone encounters a learning problem. Help students feel comfortable about indicating any learning problems they encounter. Give examples of past students succeeding even if they previously had problems in your subject area. Work at helping students believe that they are going to succeed, at having them develop an "I can do it" attitude.

The entire process of anchoring is a critical element in establishing the proper state of mind for students. Reconsider the football analogy presented earlier. Highly successful coaches help their players believe in themselves. Those coaches constantly focus on giving help to individual players when it is needed. Teaching and learning can be most effective when a teacher pays similar attention to developing comfort, challenge, and confidence in his or her students. In this author's high school, teachers in many departments brainstormed to develop resource lists of ways to anchor students at the beginning of courses. Many greeted students by shaking hands on the first day. Some developed excellent procedures for having students define class rules, rules that often were more demanding than any rules the teachers would have announced. Periodic student evaluations of teaching procedures were used in class partnerships (see the final resource section of this guide), and so on. All of this had a very visible and positive impact on the learning environment of the school. The process works as well with classes as it does with football teams.

Figure 11

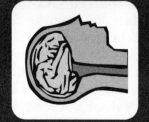

Context for the Hook

- Real-life connection
- Right-brain activity

Celebration
Challenge

Anticipation

Curiosity

Fear or apathy

Let us continue exploring factors contributing to motivation:

3. *A unique connection experience.* At the beginning of every unit you teach, some students might be in a state of fear or apathy, as shown on the first level of the steps in Figure 11. Hopefully, some of the anchoring actions described on page 21 will have lowered or even eliminated the fear level. That does not mean that the students are yet in a state of curiosity or even anticipation that leaves them wanting to learn. Your next task then is to *hook,* or connect, the students to the specific learning unit. This means that you should do something that will stimulate curiosity and a desire or anticipation for learning about the topic at hand. Figure 11 gives two helpful hints from the world of brain research. One is that you should begin by connecting the topic to real-life usefulness in some way; the brain is interested in information that has value in real life. The second is that it is usually best to provide the students with a physical experience or demonstration to make the connection to real life. This is because concrete or action-focused experiences, what some call right-brained episodes, often make a much stronger impression on the mind and on memory than do abstract, word-focused, or left-brained presentations.

We sometimes hear some educators complain about their students being apathetic or not interested enough to do homework or other tasks. More often than not, these complaints come from those who start teaching subject matter without first addressing a very important responsibility at the beginning of a teaching unit—the responsibility for a planned approach to stimulating curiosity and interest among students. Strong attention to this responsibility is the best way to combat apathy. Any teacher not already doing so should resolve now to strive to develop better and better hooks to introduce each unit he or she teaches, then keep improving the introductions from year to year. This continuous improvement project will pay great dividends in student interest.

Some of the types of activities that can be used to introduce units are:

- Unique demonstrations—The adjective *unique* is used because more dramatic, unusual, or unexpected events make a stronger impression on the brain than run-of-the-mill events. You want students to experience amazement or puzzlement, which will make them want to pay attention and learn more as they forget past fear or apathy. An example is described on page 25 of this guide.
- Simulated or "staged" events, including computer simulations.
- Visual media presentations—These are especially useful for events that are too big, too dangerous, or otherwise impossible to bring into the classroom. They should be brief.
- A relevant field trip.
- Review of a dramatic news story.
- Use of a related magic trick.
- A dramatic story or speaker—Words can sometimes "paint" dramatic images in the mind.

Figure 12

How to "Hook" Students

To begin a unit:

1. Show real-life relevance.

2. Stimulate curiosity or questions with an "experience."

Review Figure 12 to understand and practice the hook approach. Design a beginning experience to begin a unit. First, be sure the experience shows the real-life usefulness of the unit to be studied. For example, can you really imagine why a student should be interested in learning to solve quadratic equations unless he or she has some understanding of what the value of that skill might be in the real world? A few students might be interested just for the sake of getting a good grade in your course. A far greater number of early adolescents will have not yet developed executive planning skills in their prefrontal lobes to the point of thinking ahead that way. For the latter group, a more direct, here-and-now experience or demonstration of usefulness will be needed to stimulate interest. Give the class an experience that will stimulate questions, causing them to forget or move past apathy. That is how you will know if your hook is successful; it will generate spontaneous questions from students. Work on your unit introduction until that happens.

Here is an actual example of a hook used to introduce a unit on the electromagnetic spectrum in a science class:

> *Teacher*: "Let us take a look at some invisible energy that is important in your life." *Note*: There is no introductory lecture or lesson here, just a statement about *showing* something important to the students' lives.
>
> *Demonstration*: The teacher shows and turns on a rechargeable electric shaver. He or she makes sure everyone knows what it is, then holds up a small meter that will detect extremely low-frequency electromagnetic fields, an ELF meter, and states, "This meter measures electromagnetic energy of the type we are going to study. A red light will start flashing rapidly and a beeper will sound if the meter measures an amount of energy that could actually harm human tissue. Let me know if that happens, because you do not want me to be hurt."
>
> Then the teacher begins to move the operating electric shaver and the meter toward each other in front of the class. When the shaver is two or three inches from the meter, the beeper sounds and the red light flashes brightly and rapidly. At that point, the teacher holds everything in place and says, "Never hold your electric shaver closer to your face than this!"

Of course, then the questions begin and the teacher accumulates but does not yet answer them. Actual sample questions are:

- How can you use the shaver if you cannot touch it to your face safely?
- Do other devices give off this type of energy? *Note*: The students are leading toward active research projects for which you can loan them the meter.
- How do you know that this energy can harm the human body? *Note*: Some actual teaching of information might begin here with a slide or transparency showing results of research studies.

The point is that the students have all experienced an event that stimulates questions on or interest in the topic at hand. That topic is obviously something that could affect their personal well-being or health. Most will have moved past fear of science or lack of interest in science to the levels of curiosity and/or anticipation. This approach is important in any unit we offer to students.

Figure 13

Real-life Tasks

Write paragraphs that are properly constructed according to our standards and that another class member can use to program our VCR so that it automatically records the news at 6 p.m. tonight.

Write three paragraphs that are properly constructed according to our standards (with topic sentences, supporting sentences, and accurate grammar and spelling).

Now, we can move back to the list of six factors that contribute to motivation, the factors that were presented in Figure 10 on page 20. The last three factors in that figure were:

4. *Presence of useful choices.* This factor is so important that two entire sections of the guide are devoted to it. Section B-4 covers style choices. Section B-5 covers learning task choices. While postponing thorough coverage of these two topics to subsequent sections, let us fix the basic motivation principle firmly in mind right now. It is that *the human mind is usually most comfortable or least threatened by having the freedom to make useful and informed choices.* While there are many times that students will appreciate or should be given specific directions or tasks from the teacher, teachers should avoid that as their total approach. Students begin to feel threatened or even resentful if the teacher makes all their choices for them; in that instance, the teacher is taking control of their lives completely away from students. Especially if all students are always given exactly the same tasks to be pursued in the same way and on the same schedule, there is a serious danger of insensitivity to differences in learning styles and talents. It is desirable and motivating to give students reasonable choices.

5. *Curriculum perceived as relevant and useful.* By now, this guide has presented the clear message that showing students relevance and usefulness is motivating. A slight expansion of this message is that this demonstration of relevance should continue past the introduction or hook portion of a teaching unit. Figure 13 shows two different learning tasks in a language arts class. The task on the left is a traditional school/subject assignment. The assignment on the right converts this into a useful, real-life learning task that is more motivating in many ways. The practical value is clearer to students. They can have more fun measuring the quality of the results with each other. The teacher can more easily allow and encourage the use of different talents by different students—in this case, the use of drawings or labeled digital photographs incorporated into the presentation as one would often do in writing a commercial manual. Use real-life tasks whenever you can throughout an entire unit. They will increase the effectiveness of teaching and learning.

6. *Individualized support and recognition.* Again, these factors are so critical, we present them in two full sections. Section B-6 on mastery and Section B-7 on celebrating and documenting learning will provide detail. Just be aware for now that all parts of the teaching-learning system and the associated motivation factors are intertwined. Encouraging motivation takes place at all phases in the system, not just at the beginning of units.

Before proceeding to the section on choices, we shall now consider how you can prepare students to make the best use of a research-based teaching system.

Figure 14

Differences in ...

STYLES of receiving information

- Auditory
- Visual
- Somatic
- Reflective

TALENTS for processing information

- Linguistic
- Logical-Mathematical
- Visual
- Musical
- Kinesthetic
- Interpersonal
- Intrapersonal
- Naturalistic

(... From Dr. Howard Gardner's multiple intelligences)

See Section B-4.   See Section B-5.

B-3. Preparing Students

Experienced teachers—and indeed, most adults—do not need to review research studies to realize that there are style and talent differences among students. Some people like lectures; others prefer to get information from pictures or videos. Some people, such as many journalists, enjoy writing; others have more talent for musical composition. A quality teaching system depends on recognizing and adjusting to differences among students. Helping students to recognize and use the differences is a good initial step in the quality process.

Figure 14 shows partial lists of two sets of differences that we shall consider. *Styles* are different ways of receiving information. *Talents,* or what Dr. Howard Gardner calls multiple intelligences, are different ways of processing information. The same words can have different meanings in the two lists. For example, the author of this guide prefers to receive information visually from pictures and charts and videos but does not have a strong talent for producing visual patterns or representations.

Sections B-4 and B-5 cover the significance of style and talent differences for teaching in much more detail. Here, however, we address a fundamental brain principle: *The more a student knows about his or her own preferences and talents, the more he or she can use that knowledge to improve the efficiency of personal learning and problem-solving.* Students from grade 7 through high school can profit from being given instruction in style and talent differences in a schoolwide program. Afterward, they are able to use their special preferences and/or work on improving any weaknesses with less teacher direction.

Consider some examples of students knowledgeable in this area. If a student knows that he absorbs and retains visually presented information best, he may increase his use of color highlighting when reading and ask the teacher to loan him a video on a difficult topic. Another example could be a linguistically talented student volunteering to produce a poem to demonstrate her understanding of the great Civil War battle at Gettysburg (assuming the teacher is wise enough to offer choices for demonstrating learning). A third example might be a student who needs to improve his visual processing or production asking his art teacher for help and guidance with producing a picture chart for an event being covered in a history class. The concept in this latter case would be one of deliberately developing or increasing talent in some area. This is an important concept too often overlooked by the superficial approach of teaching only to strengths or preferences.

Some authors and texts might disagree with the clear separation of styles (receiving information) and talents (solving problems and producing products) into two distinct groups. This is a purely pragmatic action. It facilitates our review, especially in terms of getting students to know themselves. Just be aware that many writers and speakers mix the terms, for example, in presenting discussions of "thinking styles." In fact, we shall do some of that mixing in a preference test in the next pages.

While sections B-4 and B-5 will present suggestions on teacher use of style and talent models (one level of use of these brain models), this section is intended to encourage an equally exciting possibility—encouraging informed student use of the style and talent models (a second level of use). Let us begin by looking at a preference test for students.

Figure 15

Brain Preference Test

A
- I like learning from pictures or videos.
- I like to draw or doodle or paint.
- I can see pictures in my mind when I close my eyes.
- I like to see the "big picture" before details.
- I like to guess or imagine.
- I enjoy surprises and take risks.

B
- I love music.
- I enjoy physical activity and moving.
- When I talk, I often use hand gestures.
- I learn best from doing things.
- I like to work and talk with others.
- I like helping or teaching others.

D
- I enjoy studying science and solving problems.
- I like to follow specific directions.
- I like working with numbers.
- I like reading or writing.
- I learn well by listening.
- I do well in word games (Scrabble).

C
- I am independent (opinions).
- I have clear goals for myself.
- I enjoy working alone on a task.
- I like to practice new skills.
- I like to organize activities.
- I like to direct the work of others to get things done.

There are advantages to administering a preference test of the type shown in Figure 15 *before* teaching grade 7 through adult students about styles and talents. For instance, the answers are more apt to be free of any student attempts to make the answers support a desired conclusion. Taking and then discussing the test can also be an interest-stimulating experience or "hook" into the style and talent topics. For elementary grades, simpler surveys or oral questions and observations are usually more appropriate.

Here are the directions given to students for the test:

DIRECTIONS: Please follow these directions carefully. Circle the dot *only* for the statements that really describe you best. Then, count the number of dots circled in each quadrant—A, B, C, and D—and record the total for each in the ☐ for that quadrant. **There are no "good" or "bad" answers—only what is true for YOU.** See your counselor or teacher with any questions.

Watch the students taking the test and be ready to answer their questions. For example, on the first statement on enjoying science, a student might ask "Should I circle the dot if I like science sometimes but not other times?" The answer is, "Circle the dot *only* if the statement is almost always true about you."

This particular test is a quick and rough screening device both on preferred learning (receiving) styles and on preferred talents (multiple intelligences or thinking processes). It is useful in helping middle- and high-school students or adults begin self-analysis on personal interests and strengths and even on areas of career interest. It should not be considered conclusive in any way.

In the next pages of this section, you will find more information that will help you interpret and discuss the preference test results with your students. Please consider these recommendations in this regard:

1. Attend a workshop, study sections B-4 and B-5 of this guide, and/or do other studying on your own before you begin using the Figure 15 test or any of the commercially available preference tests in any way.

2. Caution students that the goal is not for them to just switch to a preferred style or talent when they have trouble learning or producing. Rather, it is very important to work on developing more skill in any area you do not perceive as a strength. This can give you the ability to match different styles and talents to different tasks.

3. In your school, consider using one schoolwide preference testing system with new students to avoid repetition among different classes. A student can then "own" the results and share them with each of his or her teachers.

While we have this particular test in mind, we can look at several uses. It can be helpful to both students and teachers. Remember, there are many commercial alternatives available, including some for younger students. However, this particular screening test has proven very useful in one 16-community school district.

Figure 16

Multiple Intelligences and the Preference Test

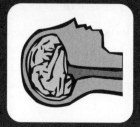

Abstract thinking

■ Linguistic
■ Logical-
   Mathematical

■ Visual
■ Musical

Sequential ─────── **Random**

■ Intrapersonal
   └ Emotional-Social
■ Naturalist

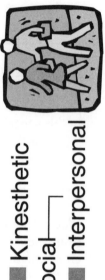

■ Kinesthetic
   └
■ Interpersonal

Experience-based thinking

The Brain Preference Test is based on a combined listing of style (receiving) and talent (processing) alternatives. While these will be explained in more detail in subsequent sections, here is a little more background information on the basis for the test.

Review Figure 16. It presents the multiple intelligences or talent basis of the four groups of test statements. As a matter of spatial convenience, the musical preference is listed on the top right quadrant. On the test itself, the one music-related statement is actually placed at the top of the lower right quadrant. This ambivalence in placement can serve as a useful reminder of several important points. The points are these:

1. No one exists totally in one quadrant of preferred activity.

2. While one person might be strong on preferences in both left quadrants and another strong in preferences in both right quadrants, many of us exhibit some preferences from all four quadrants. Of course, we increase our repertoire of ways to solve problems and create solutions as we deliberately work on increasing our range of talents. This is a critical message for students:

    > While there are real advantages to using our talent preferences and strengths, all of us can increase our personal power by deliberately working on improving our ability in multiple talent areas.

    Different problems and opportunities can best be addressed by different talents. Talents, despite being called *intelligences*, can be developed and expanded.

3. The deliberate simplicity of this short preference test means that many statements in it can relate to style or talent or both. For example, the one statement on music can relate to an enjoyable receiving activity (style) or to a creating and expressing activity (talent). In turn, creating music can have a sequential or left quadrant focus or a pattern-based right quadrant focus. The simplified screening device can serve as a stimulus to much more detailed analysis in developing useful knowledge of self.

4. At least two of the statements in the preference test are rather narrowly focused on style or receiving activity:
    a. I like to learn from pictures or videos = visual style
    b. I learn well by listening = auditory style

Once students are given a preference test, the one shown in this guide or one of the many alternatives available from other sources, help them discuss how to apply the results in their daily learning activities. The two student guides shown on the next two pages are examples of a program in one high school where all new students are given instruction on styles, talents, and other area power topics at the very beginning of grade 9. Student Guide Sheet 1 and Student Guide Sheet 2, on the next pages, are part of a ninth-grade program used to prepare students for brain-compatible learning at Minuteman Regional High School. The reflective style was not covered or introduced in this initial program.

Student Guide Sheet 1

Career Power Factor: Learning to Learn YOUR Way

1. There are different ways of receiving information; for example:

With Words	Visually	With Physical Tasks
Lectures	Videos	Building
Discussions	Movies	Fixing
Reading	Charts, diagrams, and other graphics	Moving and coordinating
	Drawing	

2. Although everyone should develop skills or styles in all of these areas, many of us learn better when receiving information in one way than in another, especially if we encounter a different learning problem.

3. One way that you can help yourself develop the strongest level of career power is to work with your counselor and teachers to discover if there is a receiving way that works best for you if you are having difficulty with a particular learning task. Ask your counselor or a teacher about the reading lab example on this.

4. Then, at appropriate times when the opportunity is available, you can switch your way or style of receiving information to gain more effectiveness. As an example, if you were experiencing a problem understanding a lecture and/or a reading on computer programming and you knew that you often function or receive best with visual help, you could ask your teacher if he or she has a video that you could watch on the topic. Or, if you learn best by doing, you could ask if the teacher could provide a combination demonstration/hands-on exercise on the programming problem.

5. The visual learning techniques are especially powerful for many of us. So look for opportunities to become familiar with and use such activities as:

   a. Mind-mapping and other graphic organizers
   b. Carefully designed underlining
   c. Combination notes:

Text notes	Picture and diagram notes

   on a divided page.

   d. Visualization

Our teachers will help you with those opportunities that can become important personalized tools as you keep learning for 40 or more years in a world of rapidly changing career information.

Student Guide Sheet 2

Career Power Factor: Capitalizing on YOUR Talents

1. There are many types of intelligences or talents. Discuss this chart of different intelligences defined from the work of Dr. Howard Gardner:

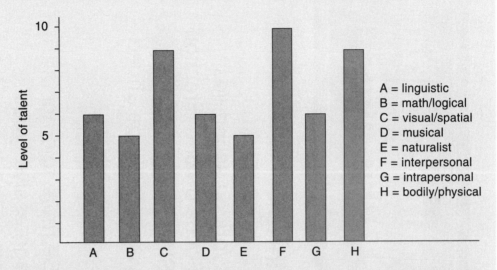

A = linguistic
B = math/logical
C = visual/spatial
D = musical
E = naturalist
F = interpersonal
G = intrapersonal
H = bodily/physical

2. A talent is a way of processing, thinking about, or using information. This is different from just receiving the information effectively. Each of us differs in our mix of the degrees of different talents or intelligences. The important question is not "How smart are you?" but rather, "How are you smart?" Work with our teachers and counselors to discover *your* answer to this important question.

3. Intelligence is the ability to solve important problems or to create useful products. So while many simplistic state or commercial tests might measure word and number "smarts" (A and B in the chart), those tests are notoriously inadequate in measuring the full range of broad practical intelligences useful in different aspects of life and in different careers. For example, if you are taking an airplane trip, you ought to hope that your flight is being guided by air-traffic controllers with a high degree of visual/spatial intelligence and not just by someone with a high score on math and literacy tests.

4. Researchers have warned legislators about the seriousness of the mistake of using one type of test to measure achievement and/or potential. However, whether these warnings are heeded or not:

   a. Do not let anyone discourage you with one type of simplistic testing.
   b. Discover your strongest talents. Our staff members can help you to do this.
   c. Match your talents to the requirement of different careers and select a career path that capitalizes on your talents.

   You can then move into a career path where you have the highest potential in spite of those who do not understand the reality of different kinds of intelligences.

5. Finally, do your best to develop and grow all of your talents, even the ones you least prefer. The different intelligences work together, not separately. So gain as much combination power and flexibility as you can for the different tasks you will face in different aspects of life and work.

Figure 17

Hints for Teachers in Certain Preference Quadrants

Abstract thinking

A
- Work on schedules
- Focus on one direction
- Slow your talk; your vision might be ahead

B
- Be more tolerant of aggressive types
- Allow individual work
- Give clear directions

D
- Soften perfectionism
- Accept randomness
- Support exploratory action

C
- Become a listener
- Pay attention to detail
- Soften your communications

Experience-based thinking

A teacher can increase the value of using a preference test by personally taking the test and using the results to broaden his or her approach to teaching methods. Our tendency as teachers is either to teach in a manner that emphasizes our personal preferences or to teach as we have been taught. Neither approach necessarily relates to all of the students in a particular classroom.

Here is a practical way to work on broadening your teaching habits:

1. Go back to page 30. Take the Preference Test in Figure 15. Record your scores (number of statements circled in each quadrant).
2. If you scored substantially higher in one or two quadrants, refer to Figure 17 for suggestions in the quadrant or quadrants in which you scored the highest.
3. Implement those suggestions in your future teaching, especially if some of your students exhibit higher scores in different quadrants than those in which you scored the highest. Your broadened teaching methods will then be more compatible with more of your students.

The next two sections will help you broaden your efforts even more.

Meanwhile, be aware that there are many more ways to use preference tests to help students use self-knowledge effectively in this area. Knowledge of personal preferences can help a student find the type of career area that he or she might enjoy the most. For example, Figure 18 shows sample career areas related to different talent preferences:

Figure 18

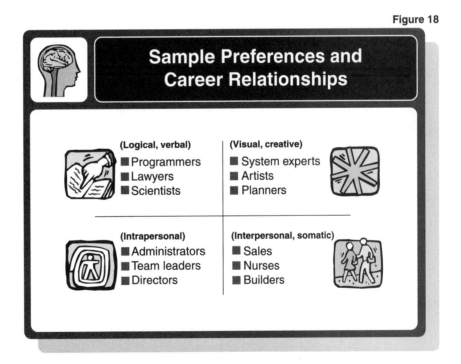

Such information can be very useful in guidance activities such as helping students explore career areas or select relevant out-of-school internships. For example, in the author's high school, career-exploration clusters are arranged in talent groups—the Technology Division for students who prefer logic, science, and mathematics; the Commercial Division for those who prefer working with people (interpersonal talent); the Construction and Power Division for students who prefer building and fixing things; and so on.

Figure 19

Some Basic Learning or Receiving Styles

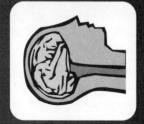

- Auditory
- Visual
- Somatic
- Reflective

B-4. Providing Style Choices

Different educators and authors list many different learning styles. Some even use the term *styles* to include thinking or processing modes. As a matter of practical choice, this guide will continue to focus on styles as ways of receiving information and on four of the most common receiving activities found in classrooms and teaching laboratories.

Figure 19 lists four of the most basic learning styles. Keep in mind that our discussing receiving information in one or more of these modes does not imply that receiving and thinking or processing are really separate activities. They usually occur together. It is just convenient and less complicated for us to analyze the receiving and processing separately before we consider them together.

Most of us and most students we teach can receive information in all four ways and indeed through many other activities not covered in this guide. There are, however, certain realities that are important to recognize to promote the most effective teaching. These realities are:

1. Some cultural, ethnic, or social groups encourage extensive use of a certain style for certain purposes. Giving a style preference test can be very useful in discovering group preferences before you begin teaching.

2. Some individuals exhibit very strong style preferences. Equipping students to use these preferences in appropriate circumstances can help them learn much more effectively. This is true for the well-researched reason previously stated in the section on motivation: the human mind is usually most comfortable or least threatened by having the freedom to make useful and informed choices. When a student prefers a certain way of receiving information and you give the students the personal opportunity and authority to make that choice, you will be promoting the student's motivation and self-confidence. When you do not provide learning style choices where that is practical, you are often increasing discomfort and diminishing self-confidence.

3. Using one's preferred style on difficult material is a useful technique. As previously mentioned, however, students should be helped to develop each style as much as possible so that they can handle situations in which they have no choice on how to receive information.

4. Visual thinking techniques can be used effectively with all four receiving styles. They are a critical but often neglected bridge between receiving and processing information. Thus, this guide emphasizes that bridge.

Keeping these facts in mind, let us look at the four basic receiving styles and the visual thinking bridge that can serve all students regardless of style preference. Please keep the entire presentation in this context: Giving style options increases learning for more students, and not giving such options decreases learning for more students. Therefore, it is difficult to imagine why anyone charged with teaching youngsters would consciously neglect the task of designing more and more style options for students over a period of years. However, there is another reality that we shall cover later in the guide: If teaching loads and federal and state focus on tests are excessive, a classroom teacher will not have time for prescribing options.

Figure 20

Common Characteristics of Auditory Learners

- Love to talk
- Loud and noisy
- Don't like paper and pencil work
- Like music, but it can distract

- Use audiotaped sessions
- Read more slowly
- Use phonics
- Use oral questions and answers
- Allow auditory experiences

Figure 20 lists common characteristics of auditory learners. Keep these qualifiers in mind. First, an auditory learner is defined as a person with a strong auditory preference; however, he or she might also like one or more other receiving styles. Second, the "common" characteristics are just that; they do not represent an exact list for any one student. For example, a student might like to talk, but he or she might also like to write. Be very careful about using a general list to attribute every characteristic in the list to any one student. Our brain systems are more complex and more individualized than that.

It is not the intent of this guide to provide many suggestions for auditory learning options. Frankly, auditory learning is all too often used to an excessive degree in many classrooms. In some secondary schools, lectures often constitute too great a portion of classroom time. For the majority of students, auditory receiving is not the most preferred receiving style. Thus, if lectures are used excessively, boredom is a common result. Material might get covered. However, telling does not guarantee learning at all.

The left side of Figure 20 lists basic characteristics. The right side lists related comments on appropriate learning activities. Sales pitches from commercial providers of learning style tests and workshops aside, you should *not* be pursuing the unrealistic task of designing individualized learning activities for each student. Rather, *the school and/or individual teachers should help individual students discover their style preferences and strengths, and individual teachers should strive to ensure that each teaching unit includes one or more auditory learning options when possible.* This approach to using students as informed managers of their own learning is what makes an option approach to teaching far more feasible and practical than it might seem at first. The teacher providing style options is the first, or Level I, approach to styles. The student being equipped to select appropriate options is the second, or Level II, approach to styles; it saves teacher time.

Here are some specific points to consider regarding the common characteristics and sample learning activities:

1. Learning activities that use discussion among students and with the teacher are an involvement improvement over lectures.

2. If a student does not like writing, that does not mean that the student and teacher can escape the need to promote development of basic writing skills. It just means that auditory learning should be included as a part of the mix of options.

3. Be careful with the use of music. It can promote better learning through exciting introductions, as part of learning celebrations, as signals for a change of pace, and in some cases as a calming background for study or memorization. However, for some auditory learners (perhaps 7 to 10 percent of some groups), background music presents a severe distraction that generates frustration. Be sure to give students the opportunity to ask that background music be eliminated if it bothers them. Teach your students to speak to you on such matters. Study and attend a course or workshop with an expert before you begin any use of background music.

4. The use of audiotapes can be a useful library and loan resource for those students who enjoy auditory learning. Of course, videotapes also include the audio component for combined-style home use.

Figure 21

Comparison of H.S. Reading Lab Students
(All 3.5 or more years below grade level in reading on entering grade 9)

N = 14 = 25 hours in lab
no
auditory training

Average grade level
gain per hour in lab
= .177

N = 10 = 25 hours in lab
+ 40 hours in
auditory training*

Average grade level
gain per hour in lab
= .216

* Auditory learning program: Fast ForWord for Middle/High School from Scientific Learning

Before leaving the discussion of auditory style, let us consider a reverse situation. There are students who have auditory discrimination problems. This is the exact opposite of preferring auditory learning. Worse, research by cognitive scientists indicates that there is a relationship between auditory discrimination problems and lower reading skills. Some students simply cannot separate the sounds they are hearing well enough to engage in proper word recognition, even after receiving traditional phonics instruction. This lowers their ability to listen effectively and even to read efficiently as the mental sequence of converting sounds or silent sounding to words to related mental images is then inadequate.

Figure 21 summarizes the results from a short experiment with two groups of students entering grade 9. All students in both groups scored 3.5 or more years below grade level in their total score on a Metropolitan Achievement Test. All were placed in a computer-based reading lab program that allowed them to select different learning styles and to proceed at different rates. However, the 10 students in the group shown on the left were concurrently enrolled in a special computer-based training program on auditory discrimination for 10 weeks. The 14 students in the group shown on the right were not given the special auditory training program. At the end of the 10-week auditory program, the students in that program exhibited an average 22 percent higher gain per hour of time spent in the reading lab. The use of a gain-per-hour average comparison is a way of accounting for the fact that some students spent more time than others in the reading lab. Students in the auditory training program also described other benefits, such as "My teachers talk slower now." Of course, since there was no change in teachers' talk, this student was describing the fact that he could now understand what they were saying better. His decoding process had been "tuned" and accelerated.

The auditory program used in this experiment was Middle and High School software from Scientific Learning. For 48 minutes every weekday for 10 weeks, the students in the program engaged in exercises that accelerated their ability to discriminate sounds (phonological fluency), recognize and remember words, and answer questions on stories. Visible records of progress helped to motivate the participants in an accelerated learning environment skillfully managed by two enthusiastic teachers. The company's research on this software includes magnetic resonance images showing higher levels of activity in more areas of the brain as training progresses. This is a classic case of showing why *we should help students increase their style abilities* and not just always seek to use preferred styles. The experiment also illustrates a point that we shall emphasize later in this guide: The importance of using analyzed data to make instructional decisions. The data from this experiment and experiments in other schools helped school officials decide to purchase and to plan expansion of the use of this software.

This is the right place to emphasize another point on styles (and later on talents). The point is: *Various styles and other brain functions are interrelated; they are not separate entities.* For example, in this case, improving auditory discrimination, or the ability to use the auditory receiving style, leads to improvement in visualizing words, or the visual function associated with reading. There are now programs from several firms based on research documenting reading gains and even changed brain images; they use intensive sound training and/or multisensory exercises to improve reading ability far more effectively than classic once-a-week remedial sessions. Students and parents should be helped to become aware of the power of such researched relationships as we give them one of the greatest gifts of effective schooling—learning how to learn.

Figure 22

Common Characteristics of Visual Learners

- Notice things
- Look first; directions if needed
- Not good at phonics but some can be speed readers
- Like pictures, color, charts

- Use vivid language
- Underline, map, highlight
- Seek patterns
- Use visual cues
- Encourage drawing along with written notes
- Use charts, videos

Figure 22 lists some common characteristics of visual learners. These are students with a strong visual preference for receiving information. Again, this preference might be combined with a strong preference for another style such as hands-on learning. In one high school where students who elected vocational-technical programs were given a preference test on entry, approximately 90 percent described a strong preference for visual, hands-on, or a combination of those two learning styles. Indeed, many students entered the vocational-technical programs because of dissatisfaction with school programs that were, for them, excessively focused on words and abstraction. In the proper learning environment that recognized and used their preferred learning styles, many of these students exhibited talents and achievements that marked them as superior learners. Of course, nearly every school has a significant population of students who learn best from visual and hands-on experiences. If this fact is ignored, three words apply: poor teaching practice.

The left side of Figure 22 lists basic characteristics. The right side lists related comments on appropriate learning activities. Again, the important implications are:

1. Help individual students discover their learning styles.
2. Provide visual options for receiving information.
3. Teach skills that will enable students to use visual learning on their own.

The third point is especially important. Students can be taught to use brain-mapping to take notes. They can be encouraged to use highlighters on written materials that do not have to be returned to the school. They can be shown how to use graphic organizers effectively to seek and even create patterns of relationships, something we shall cover in more detail in the next section on talents or thinking styles.

It is especially important *not* to consider brain-mapping as a tool only for students with a visual learning style preference. Rather, this visual tool of a key word, icon, or concept surrounded by knowledge branches to main points and subtopics can be very useful for most students regardless of their learning styles.

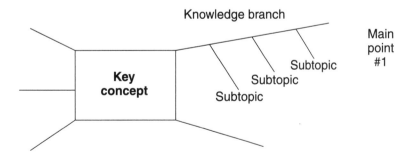

When you are engaged in auditory receiving, if the speaker to whom you are listening shifts points, or if you, the listener, want to relate a new point to an old point, it is easier to record the shift or relationship on a visual map without losing your auditory focus. If you are a kinesthetic learner, the action of drawing or physically tracing concepts on a visual map of notes is also helpful for memory storage.

There are many good books and videos available on brain-mapping. See the resource section for catalogs that list some examples. Every teacher should learn mapping and should help students learn and use mapping effectively. Later in the guide, we shall discuss the cause and effect as a form of brain-mapping.

Figure 23

Common Characteristics of Somatic Learners

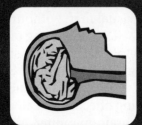

- Use gestures
- Like physical activity
- Dislike sitting still
- Do not like emphasis on abstraction
- Some are kinesthetic and some tactile

- Allow movement and interaction
- Work with material
- Learn by doing
- Use projects
- Provide interactive computer programs

Figure 23 shows common characteristics of somatic learners. Again, the left side lists typical behavior or preferences. The right side suggests types of useful or related learning activities. For example, learning games that involve movement, construction of models, field trips, and use of computer programs that involve selecting or moving components on the screen can all be very motivating and productive for somatic learners.

In the English for the Entrepreneur class at Minuteman Regional High School, a teacher and his students conducted a simple experiment on this. They selected a relatively boring task—learning the names and functions of muscles in the arm. A standard approach of reading, studying pictures, and just attempting to memorize the name and function of each muscle area identified by the teacher gave very poor results. When individual students were asked to name and describe the function of each muscle, most students gave wrong answers more often than correct answers. The class then switched to a well-designed movement and descriptive chanting exercise. The patterned movement combined with coordinated chanting of names and functions rapidly led to very good results. When individual students then were asked to name and describe the functions of the muscles, most gave correct answers more often than wrong answers. The same positive test results were repeated after one month and several months later. When asked about the muscles, the learners immediately touched the area named and recalled the chant and then the correct information. They had experienced a powerful learning alternative.

The message here is not that movements and chanting are better ways to learn. Rather, we need to recognize that there are many ways to learn. Teaching students to discover and use their learning style preferences and then providing learning style options in every class is good teaching practice.

Two major cautions are appropriate at this point:

1. It is not a reasonable practice to give every student a learning style test and then attempt to assign individualized learning activities to each student. That approach is too complex and time-consuming to be at all practical. The reasonable approach is to help students become aware of different ways of learning and to give them options whenever possible. In life after school, they will be expected to use different learning styles in different situations.

2. A teacher or trainer should be very careful to avoid unnecessary forcing of a disliked learning option on a student. You have probably experienced a workshop on creative teaching in which the leader was a fanatic about movement games or social interaction, one exercise after another. Watch the participants carefully. Some become truly alienated as a type of learning they dislike is repeated. Sometimes with adults you can hear the groans ("not another game!") or watch some participants disappear from the workshop at the break. Teachers and trainers who are insensitive to this can have a devastating impact, especially on grade 9–12 students, who normally cannot disappear from the class.

Before moving to the final "bridging" learning style, point 1 above deserves even more emphasis here. That point is that *a teacher's major goal should be to present relevant learning style options to students.* The goal should not be to prescribe learning style *X* for student *Y* except in two cases. The first case would be when you want to develop a particular learning style skill for everyone or a style that is

Figure 24

Common Characteristics of Reflective Learners

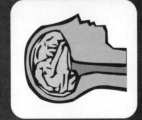

- May exhibit a preference for one or more other receiving styles, but ...
- Especially enjoy discovering or constructing new information on their own

- Use "discovery" assignments in which students investigate or do research to define their own conclusions, rules, hypotheses, or products = receiving new information from personal thinking necessary for a specific task. The second case would occur when a student is encountering a learning problem and you wish to suggest a style approach that might help solve the problem. Again, a major part of the secret to effective teaching is presentation of variety in learning options.

Figure 24 refers to reflective learners—those who work at constructing new information themselves. Now we shall review our last major learning style: reflective learning. Many authors and workshop presenters do not list this style; they often concentrate on the auditory, visual, and somatic styles only. However, since this book defines style as a way of receiving information, we should recognize that the human brain system can use thinking as a way to create and thus receive information. This style, then, can be called a "bridge" between receiving information and the thinking or talent options we shall review in the next section.

Figure 24 presents a simple description of the style preference in the left-hand column and a very general description of the learning activity in the right-hand column. Since using thinking to produce information clearly depends on using other styles first (that is, you gain information from reading, observing, and so on, and then reflect on that information), we normally do not label a person as a reflective learner. Rather, the major advice for teaching is that we should encourage *every* student to use reflection to construct information. Literally hundreds of excellent books are available on encouraging critical thinking skills. On the most practical level this means that every teaching/learning unit should include or culminate with activities that require each student to move from just receiving information through the senses to creating information with thinking processes. This creation can be demonstrated through products such as a paper analyzing causes, a defended or tested hypothesis, a physical model or machine designed by the student, an original presentation to others, or a poem that is a new expression of feelings or impressions. Before we move to the thinking or talent or "intelligence" options that are an important part of needed variety in teaching and learning activity, let us look at a simplified diagram of where we are now in reviewing a teaching system:

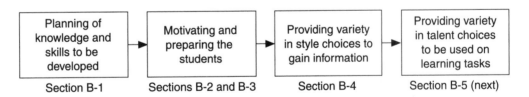

| Planning of knowledge and skills to be developed | Motivating and preparing the students | Providing variety in style choices to gain information | Providing variety in talent choices to be used on learning tasks |
| Section B-1 | Sections B-2 and B-3 | Section B-4 | Section B-5 (next) |

Before proceeding to Section B-5, be sure that you understand each previous section in the system.

Figure 25

Multiple Intelligences
Based on the Work of Dr. Howard Gardner

1. Linguistic intelligence
2. Mathematical-Logical intelligence
3. Visual-Spatial intelligence
4. Musical intelligence
5. Kinesthetic intelligence
6. Interpersonal intelligence
7. Intrapersonal intelligence
8. Naturalistic intelligence
9. Philosophical-Ethical intelligence

B-5. Providing Learning Task or Talent Choices

Figure 25 lists talents, or intelligences, from the multiple intelligences model developed by Dr. Howard Gardner of Harvard University. Go back to pages 32 and 33 to refresh your memory on how these talents or ways of thinking are related to the Preference Test presented earlier in this guide. If you need a refresher summary, read Student Guide Sheet 2 on page 35 again. Be aware that the earlier pages in this guide do not refer to intelligences 8 and 9 as listed in Figure 25. These are the last two intelligences that Dr. Gardner added to his evolving model as this guide was produced. Also, be aware that other researchers and authors describe other models with other named intelligences. This guide uses Dr. Gardner's model because it is so well known and so practical. Remember that a model is a hypothetical representation of reality, a representation that is most useful if it helps us to make accurate predictions. Dr. Gardner's model recognizes a clear reality—that different people possess different talents or problem-solving abilities (i.e., intelligences) to different degrees. By describing the talents and relating them to value in different tasks, powerful learning principles can be defined and pursued.

In the previous section on styles, we ended with the recommendation that we should encourage every student to use reflection or thinking to produce new information or products. Indeed, the multiple intelligences model views intelligence as a talent that enables a person to solve problems or create new products. A student who can use information to solve problems is a student who is demonstrating the highest level of learning.

The important point in this section is to be aware of and to use the fact that different individuals have different talent strengths. Einstein said that he liked to think first in pictures—to visualize hypotheses and solutions. Many young people with high visual talent feel discouraged if a teacher places excessive emphasis on words, numbers, and logic in a way that fails to give them an opportunity to demonstrate artistic skills or the power of their visionary creativity. Many young people with physical skills can learn and solve problems best when allowed to build and/or physically try solutions. To regularly impose learning tasks that emphasize only one or two talents is somewhat akin to insisting that all of the students wear the same size shoe regardless of the sizes of their feet.

Remember, now, we have changed from discussing styles of receiving information to talents or ways of processing and using information. So, the learning tasks discussed here are assignments in which students are expected to use critical skills to produce products or to solve problems. As with learning styles, we need to introduce variety in this area so that students can pursue two goals:

1. Have the opportunity to develop different talents, since any talent or intelligence can be improved. (The concept of fixed intelligence is completely obsolete.)

2. Have the opportunity to use a preferred talent as a matter of motivation and possible career interest.

Any teacher or trainer who does not provide some options in production or problem-solving assignments is not facilitating the pursuit of these two important goals described.

Figure 26

Principles for Using Different Intelligences or Talents

1. Teach the "How are you smart?" philosophy.

2. Ensure opportunities to pursue tasks with preferred talents.

3. Teach the fact that the intelligences work together, not separately.

4. Give opportunities for each student to develop numerous talents.

The principles of using the multiple intelligences, or talents, model are shown in Figure 26. Here are some comments on each of these principles:

1. *Teach the "How are you smart?" philosophy.* The concept of intelligence as a simple fixed characteristic or as an answer to the question "How smart are you?" is completely obsolete. It is important that Student Guide Sheet 2, shown on page 35, be thoroughly reviewed with students so that they are helped to reject the obsolete concept and to seek their own talent strengths.

2. *Ensure opportunities to pursue tasks with preferred talents.* Simple surveys like the preference test, covered on pages 30 and 31, can help students become aware of their preferences. Then a teacher's job is to construct and offer task options in learning units, options that allow students to pursue problem solving with different talents or by using a combination of talents. Sample options are presented beginning on pages 54 and 55.

3. *Teach the fact that the intelligences work together, not separately.* On pages 42 and 43, an experiment with teaching auditory discrimination skills was described. Improving these skills led to improvement on visual reading tasks. Some teachers have found that teaching visual-spatial skills leads to improved ability to solve problems in mathematics.[2] The latter result is not surprising, since being able to visualize a problem can certainly be helpful in applying logical analysis to the problem. In simple terms, be sure that students understand that complex problems are usually best solved with multiple thinking approaches rather than with any one intelligence.

4. *Give opportunities for each student to develop numerous talents.* Once point 3 is understood, you can and should expect students to work on learning tasks that emphasize the need for using a talent or intelligence that is not a preference. Real-world tasks often require a specific talent. Thus, one legitimate goal of education is to develop each talent to the greatest possible degree with each student.

A special historical comment is in order here before we review some sample tasks that can be associated with different talents. In past decades, schools, colleges, and test publishers have made the mistake of emphasizing two areas of talent, or intelligence, over the others. The two traditional areas are linguistic intelligence and mathematical-logical intelligence. Approximately 15 years ago, neuroscience and cognitive research began to move educators and policymakers toward a broadened approach—giving more recognition to the value of other intelligences. That broadened approach helped more youngsters gain respect for and confidence in their nontraditional intelligences. It also increased economic viability, since many different career paths are dependent on far more than two of the many different talents. Now national and state accountability laws have renewed the narrow emphasis on the two traditional intelligences. There is nothing inherently wrong with measuring growth in the two traditional talents. They are important. However, when that is done without concurrent attention to other talents, that is a form of misguided elitism and discrimination. Concerned educators and parents and informed employees should focus on correcting this repetition of a past mistake, especially when narrow tests are used for graduation purposes.

---

2. David Thornburg, at a seminar in Sturbridge, Massachusetts, October 26, 1991, describing his wife's experiment in teaching visual skills to third graders working on a mathematics unit.

Teacher Guide Sheet 1

Sample Learning Tasks for Different Talents

Intelligence or Talent	Sample Types of Learning Tasks	
1. Linguistic	• Reading and analyzing	• Presenting
	• Writing reports	• Debating
2. Mathematical-logical	• Planning and budgeting	• Discovering patterns
	• Comparing or classifying	• Calculating
3. Visual-spatial	• Using paper and charts	• Designing
	• Preparing visual representations	• Decorating
4. Musical	• Composing music or songs	• Using musical cues
	• Playing an instrument	• Using voice inflection and tones
5. Kinesthetic	• Constructing	• Using equipment
	• Competing physically	• Examining and analyzing
6. Interpersonal	• Working with others (teaming)	• Sharing with others
	• Interviewing	• Responding to others
7. Intrapersonal	• Directing one's self	• Exercising leadership
	• Analyzing personal feelings and goals	• Reflecting and reporting on personal experiences
8. Naturalistic	• Investigating and reporting on nature	• Classifying materials
	• Planning and doing a science experiment	• Designing an environmental protection plan
9. Philosophical-ethical	• Establishing a mission • Commenting on philosophy of political leaders	• Designing a class code of ethics • Comparing the moral views of different groups

Comments: The goal in each unit can be to give two or three learning task or production choices, except when you intend to have every student exhibit and develop the same talent. Clearly, most reasonably complex real-world tasks will also cut across two or more talent areas. Also, group or team projects can be designed to allow different team members to make different talent contributions.

Teacher Guide Sheet 1 on page 54 lists generic types of learning or production tasks that relate strongly to specific intelligences or talents. The exact detail of using a specific suggestion will depend on the subject and grade, age, or experience level of the students or trainees in a class. The important point again is that *we should deliberately give students task options that allow them to use their individual talents. We should also work carefully at helping all students develop talents that might not represent their strengths or preferences.* In this process, you can help students appreciate the need for developing all talents by emphasizing that the intelligences work together. We separate them in order to define and analyze them, not because they operate independently. Finally, it is important to emphasize that *each intelligence can be grown or strengthened.* There are many fine books and manuals available on activities that do just that—increase a specific talent. The most versatile problem solvers in our world are those who work at developing each of their intelligences. They are then able to use the intelligences that are most effective in different situations.

Two intelligence areas deserve special attention here. First, today's youngsters have grown up in a world of visual messages. Television and multimedia communication have helped to wire stronger brain circuits for visual processing or thinking. In working with contemporary students, many teachers using the system in this guide have found graphic organizers to be especially effective at promoting strong thinking processes. For example, the cause-and-effect diagram provides a powerful visual framework for analyzing and solving problems; it is a form of brain-mapping:

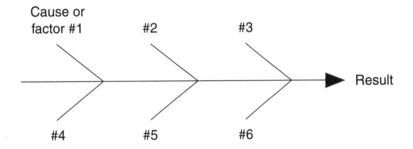

More information and samples on this are presented in Section B-6.

Second, there are a significant number of students who can profit from more physical activity in their learning tasks. Physical activity stimulates circulation, motivates kinesthetic learners, and can improve learning, since the mind and body work together rather than separately. Learning games and tasks involving physical activity, combined with the use of other talents, can be powerful. Teachers and trainers add an important dimension to the effectiveness of their instruction when they carefully add some physical learning tasks to their options.

Finally, *it is important for schools to help students improve their emotional intelligence.* Emotional intelligence is really a combination of the interpersonal and intrapersonal intelligences working together. It is an important combination that often determines whether a person succeeds in working with others and in gaining promotions on a career path. Strong linguistic or mathematical intelligences alone are rarely adequate for career success if the products of those intelligences are communicated in a way that alienates team members in the workplace. Teacher Guide Sheet 2, shown on pages 56 and 57, provides basic information on this topic.

Teacher Guide Sheet 2

Emotional Intelligence—An Important Talent for Every Student

There are many types of intelligences and learning styles. Students and teachers who use this reality can do the most to develop full career potential. In this guide, we consider emotional intelligence by giving answers to five questions.

Question #1 is, *Why is emotional intelligence important?* The powerful answer is that a person's emotional intelligence, or EI, is often the most important factor in determining success or failure in a career path. Putting aside downsizing in a weakening economy, more employees are fired or fail to gain promotions because they have failed to develop their EI than for any other reason. Students who work at developing their EI make a wonderful contribution to their future success.

Question #2 is, *What is emotional intelligence?* It is a person's ability to deal with his or her own emotions and the emotions of others in a constructive manner, a manner that promotes teamwork and productivity rather than conflict. Perhaps most importantly, it is an ability that can be taught and "grown," just like the other intelligences that we shall review in future articles.

Question #3 is, *How can you recognize emotional intelligence?* The most direct way to answer this is to describe what you will see if a person is exhibiting a high level of the five basic components of EI. The person will show these skills:

1. **Self-awareness**—The person recognizes his or her emotions and their causes. In effect, he or she is an observer of self who can make clear and informed decisions about personal action.

2. **Self-regulation**—The person, armed with self-awareness, controls his or her actions carefully, rather than just reacting to a situation solely on the basis of impulse generated by an emotion-generating event. (This is not a matter of denying or hiding emotions, but rather of not being ruled by emotions.)

3. **Self-motivation**—When something goes wrong, the high-EI person does not ask, "What is wrong with me (or us)?" He or she asks, "What can I (or we) fix?"

4. **Empathy**—The person exhibits interest and an ability in recognizing the feelings of others. Empathy gives one the ability to "walk in the other person's shoes."

5. **Effective relationships**—Using the previously listed four skills, the person communicates with others in a way that addresses their needs as well as his or her own needs. The emphasis is on solving problems together, not unnecessary confrontation. The high-EI person communicates with a constructive goal in mind.

Of course, the opposite of high EI is not difficult to recognize. If you are exposed to a coworker or student who is highly emotional and quick to act on his or her emotions, with little or no sensitivity to the feelings of others, you know that coworker's or student's communications often tend to hurt or antagonize others. As more and more companies perceive their dependence on good teaming among employees and on earning the goodwill of customers who will not tolerate rudeness, these companies are seeking workers with high EI and implementing training to improve the EI skills of existing employees.

Question #4 is, *When and how can we develop high emotional intelligence?* The so-called window or optimum period for developing strong emotional intelligence is from birth through adolescence. This means that the high-school years give a critical last chance to develop these skills that will be a major factor in career success or failure. Teachers who deal constructively with their own emotions and who show respect for their students' feelings, but who deliberately require students to perceive how their behavior is affecting others, are encouraging the development of strong EI. Schools that train staff members to support this growth process and build EI development exercises throughout existing courses make a major contribution to the career success potential of students. Excellent curriculum resource materials are readily available to help teachers in this area.

Question #5 is, *How can you promote growth of emotional intelligence in your school?* Students and teachers can:

1. Hold discussions to become fully aware of the power and principles of EI.
2. Practice implementing EI power every day—in class interactions, in peer discussions, in the cafeteria, at home, everywhere.
3. Evaluate each person's contribution to person-to-person exchange with these questions:
   a. Did he or she control personal emotions adequately?
   b. Did he or she show sensitivity to and concern for the feelings of others?
   c. Did he or she exhibit persistence in wanting to improve personal performance?
   d. Did he or she deliberately seek to team or to solve problems rather than to confront or hurt others?
   e. Did he or she take pride in and celebrate the constructive use of EI?

. . . all without abandoning principles of character such as honesty, fairness, helpfulness, and the right to personal safety and dignity.

Figure 27

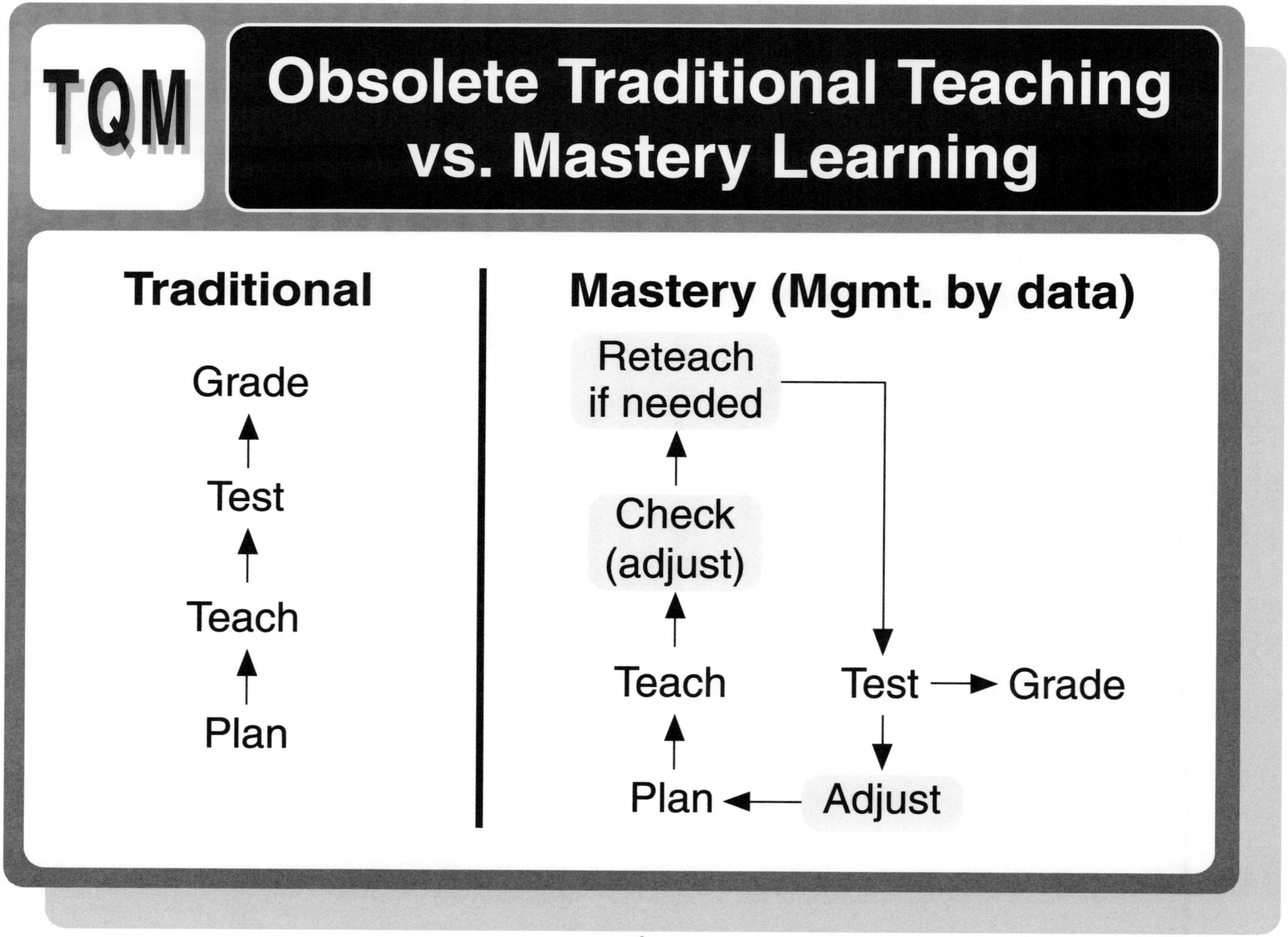

TQM

Obsolete Traditional Teaching vs. Mastery Learning

Mastery (Mgmt. by data)

Reteach if needed → Test → Grade

Plan → Teach → Check (adjust) → Reteach if needed

Plan → Adjust

Traditional

Plan → Teach → Test → Grade

B-6. Promoting Mastery with Data

In its simple traditional form, teaching consists of planning what to teach, teaching it, then testing students and giving each one a grade. That process is obsolete; it leads to normal curve grades of A, B, C, D, and F. In our competitive global economy, C and D achievement levels are simply not competitive.

Review Figure 27. Compare the mastery process on the right to the traditional process on the left. Three critical elements have been added in the mastery process:

1. At a *Check and adjust* stage, students are given formative (not-for-grade) tests to see if they have learned desired knowledge and/or skills.

2. Then, if a student has not learned some information or skill, you adjust by *Reteaching* that student, using different methods, tasks, or styles of learning if necessary. The goal in this critical step is to have the student achieve mastery, not to be content with a grade of F, D, or C. Depending on time and the critical nature of competencies that need to be addressed, reteaching might even be done more than once. The purpose of teaching is mastery to the degree possible, not bland acceptance of some students mastering skills and some students not mastering important skills.

3. Once teaching and reteaching have been completed and a test-for-grade (summative test) has been used to issue grades or celebrate issuance of competency certificates, the *Adjust* step is continued. In this phase, data on student achievement are used to determine what part of your teaching plan worked with whom and what you could do to improve the teaching plan for the future. You then adjust your teaching plan.

We shall provide more information on the adjusting and celebration processes in sections B-7 and B-8.

In previous sections of the guide, through Section B-5, we reviewed different styles and talent or intelligence tasks that could be used in the reteaching process. Peer tutoring, extra help sessions, and many other alternatives can also be used. While some students are being retaught critical skills, students who have mastered those skills can either help with the reteaching process or pursue extra learning alternatives that give them expanded and stronger skill backgrounds. Be sure that any extra tasks are opportunities for more growth or for projects of personal interest to students. You do not want successful learning to be "punished" by earning boring or disagreeable assignments!

This section will emphasize the collection, analysis, and use of data in a good teaching system. The data are intended to be a tool for pursuing mastery by students.

First, be aware that the use of data should be related to your becoming familiar with research on teaching and learning methods. On the next two pages, we consider some simple research on time. Once you become aware of this research, you can design a teaching schedule that applies it. Then you can measure whether or not the application improves results and adjust future teaching accordingly. You are on your way to true management of learning. Every teacher faces a basic choice here. A teacher can just give information and correct assignments, or a teacher can constantly manage improvement of the teaching-learning process.

Figure 28

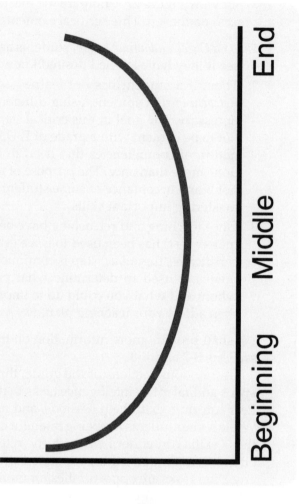

Again, there is a traditional practice in schools—a tendency to focus on accumulating data on the results of instruction. We begin this section by suggesting that there is a need to go beyond results data, to study relationships between results and information on students and teaching processes. If students in two high schools achieve an equal average score on state tests but the students in one school started at much lower achievement levels, the processes in the two schools are not equal. The school that started with students at lower achievement levels added the most value to student achievement; its teaching processes are more effective.

As managers of learning, teachers should study the effectiveness of different processes. Consider just one factor as an example—the use of research on time. There is a large body of experimentation on time reported in the literature. Two clear principles emerge from these studies:

1. *More learning normally occurs at the beginning and at the end of a learning activity than in the middle of the activity.* Refer to Figure 28. Various authors give this principle different names—the BEM (beginning-end-middle) principle, the primary and recency theory, and so on. The message is simple: Do not regularly pursue one unvarying learning activity for an excessive length of time. There are exceptions for less intense or some hands-on activities.

2. *The brain's attentiveness is aided by alternating periods of focused learning and either breaks or a less intense learning activity.* The length of the intense or focused learning can be longer with adults, perhaps 25 minutes or so. It should be shorter for elementary youngsters, not more than 10 minutes. The focus period for high-school students can be 15 to 20 minutes.

A teacher can experiment with different patterns of alternating lectures, application exercises, discussions, breaks, and reviews in a unit from one year or class to the next. Results from different patterns can be measured, analyzed, and discussed with students to help determine the pattern that works best for a specific unit. Many teachers in Minuteman Regional High School have found that the following pattern works well for many units:

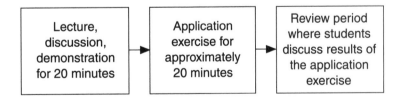

This pattern fits into a 60-minute period and is followed by the between-class break or passing period. It is the pattern that proved so effective in the English for the Entrepreneur class described on pages 4 and 5 of this guide.

The major point to remember here is that you are using data to evaluate improvement in instructional techniques, not just to give grades to students. We shall provide more examples of this in the remainder of this section.

Figure 29

TQM

Deming's Profound Knowledge for Pursuing Continuous Improvement

1. **SYSTEMS** support quality.

2. **MODELS** provide the basis for improving service. (Brain research)

3. **MEASUREMENT TOOLS** are needed to guide improvement.

4. **TEAMING** is the "secret ingredient" in improvement.

Adapted from Dr. W. Edwards Deming

Did you notice the changed logo in the upper left corner of the last three figures—the letters *TQM* instead of a brain? The new logo stands for Total Quality Management. Figure 29 summarizes what Dr. W. Edwards Deming called his "profound knowledge" principles for pursuing improving results in any enterprise, including education. In this book we are using *TQM* to remind you of these points, even though that acronym does not come from Deming:

1. *Total* refers to the need to involve everyone in a school in a *team* approach to pursuing quality. The system presented in this guide has maximum impact when every staff member and every student is dedicated to implementing the principles of profound knowledge.
2. *Quality*, as we use the term, refers to *continuous improvement in measured results.*
3. *Management* refers to the *use of data* to guide improvement efforts.

The previous sections of this guide concentrated on the use of a brain-research model in a system approach to teaching. This section concentrates on the measurement tools that the staff-student team can use to guide improvement. The profound knowledge principles and the TQM reminder can help you stay focused on the total system approach to quality or continuous improvement in education. Do not get lost in the definitions. Understand that what you are really doing is managing a process to convert the obsolete "normal" curve of student achievement into an improved curve of student achievement something like this:

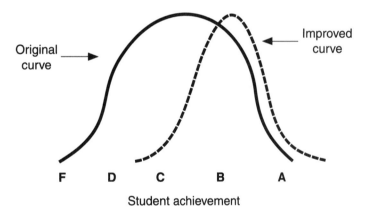

Some initial state and national testing procedures recognize the important point here—that *quality is a direction, a movement toward improvement.* However, those procedures are not well done if they establish absolute scores that do not consider students starting at different entry points and having different learning styles and rates. Educators should insist on improvement toward a value-added approach to state and national assessment, an approach in which teachers are recognized for promoting growth. Otherwise, our nation would be tolerating the misuse of statistical analysis.

Figure 30

Context for Data Management

TQM

A. An analogy

- Medical data → Doctor
- Learning data → Teacher

B. Using data in teaching

Limited use
- Giving grades.

Good use
- What learning already exists?
- How is new learning progressing?
- What works best?
- Giving grades.

Figure 30 presents an analogy as a final context for managing with data. Most of us want a physician who is treating us to accumulate these data:

1. Symptoms and indicators of our current condition and needs
2. Implications of research of our condition and improvement
3. Impact of specific treatment, including indications of the need for alternative treatment or referral

This is all so logical that it does not seem to need elaboration or discussion.

Learning is a process of the human body, as are our other biological processes. Therefore, anyone concerned with promoting a healthy learning process should logically accumulate these data:

1. Symptoms and indicators of each student's current learning status and needs. (Is the student reading on grade level? What are the student's learning style strengths and weaknesses?)
2. Implications of research for each student's state of learning and improvement. (Is the student ready for the next level in mathematics, or are there critical skills missing? In what ways might the student learn best?)
3. Impact of a specific teaching-learning sequence and indications of the need for alternative learning opportunities or referral.

Can there be any doubt that the use of data is just as important in education as it is in medical practice? Do any of us want our youngsters being taught by educators who do not use data wisely any more than we would want to be treated by physicians who do not bother to use relevant data wisely? Failure to use data properly in either the field of medicine or the field of education constitutes malpractice.

Notice the words *wisely*, *relevant*, and *properly* in the previous sentences. This guide is not intended to encourage the indiscriminate use of data. It is not intended to suggest toleration of misuse of data, as in the case of using absolutes instead of value-added measurements. Every educator has the professional obligation to learn and to practice the fundamentals of good data analysis. Those fundamentals are not complicated. They are a necessary part of an effective teaching system.

The next few pages review the fundamentals of the use of data analysis and present simple or generic examples. No one needs a course in statistics to use the techniques. The resource section lists materials any educator can use to gain additional knowledge and capabilities. The resource section also provides examples of useful software. Keep in mind that newer and better software products are produced every year. Therefore, it is useful for any school or district to assign someone the responsibility of reviewing and reporting on new data analysis products annually. Such products should provide the type of analysis you decide is most useful and, when purchased, should be supported with a strong initial training program and annual orientation for new staff members. There is no excuse for requiring individual teachers to learn every new program on their own.

Figure 31

TQM

How Data Can Help

1. Measure student achievement
2. Identify those falling behind and allow reteaching
3. Measure effectiveness of teaching and process approaches
4. Guide students and parents
5. Disclose root causes of problems
6. Promote accountability (state and federal laws)
7. Guide continuous improvement

Each school, district, and even individual staff members must decide what data are relevant and useful. Figure 31 provides a partial list of generic ways in which data can be helpful. It might be useful for you to make a copy of this list and refer to it as we look at sample examples of data analysis. Place a check beside the type of help that an example seems to provide. Add to the list as you discover new ways that data might help in your classroom, department, or school.

Looking at the list in Figure 31, consider these comments on specific numbered items:

1. Measuring student achievement is the traditional use of data. Such data become far more useful if you also measure:
   a. Individual and class trends
   b. The relationship of achievement to such factors as previous achievement of students, attendance, homework completion, and so on. In other words, you seek reasons for achievement or lack of achievement.
2. A primary use of data is identifying students who need extra help and reteaching to reach mastery.
3. When we try new programs or techniques, we should try to answer this question: Did they lead to an improvement in learning?
4. Analysis of individual and class data is absolutely necessary in order to give solid guidance in student or parent conferences. Is student *X* failing, or is most of the class not learning effectively? Can we discover the reason(s) for either reality?
5. Can we discover relationships between a certain factor and student achievement? For example, are low scores on state mathematics tests highly correlated with levels of reading ability?
6. Can we show which students succeed and which ones fail on selected types of state test items related to specific learning strands in a required curriculum framework? Can we then change our curriculum in a way that leads to improved future results?
7. Can students and teachers learn to use data together to promote continuous improvement in both individual and total class learning? Effective use of data in items 1 through 6 naturally leads to an affirmative answer in item 7.

The seven-item list is not fully inclusive. For example, it does not address such items as evaluating peer assistance among professional staff members. Every support and service department should certainly accumulate and use customer satisfaction and suggestion data. When such data are used, teachers can benefit from continuous improvement in service to them. This can then translate indirectly into improved service to students. This returns us to the word *total* and the fundamental concept that improved service based on data analysis should be a responsibility in every component of a school organization. This guide is simply intended to stimulate action on the responsibility. It cannot provide examples for every department and service.

Figure 32

TQM

Types of Data Related to Students

1. **Input variables** (reading level, special needs, previous learning, learning styles, etc.)

2. **Process variables** (teaching systems, materials, time options, support structures)

3. **Output variables** (competencies achieved, tests passed, placement, etc.)

The mastery, check/adjust, and celebrate/document components of the teaching system are intertwined in an order that is not strictly sequential. We shall return to clarify this in sections B-8 and B-9 but will continue now with a discussion of data and data analysis to keep most direct comments on that topic in one section.

There are three broad categories of data that can be helpful. These data categories are summarized in Figure 32 in relation to students:

1. *Input variables.* What previous learning (or lack thereof) and special needs does each student bring to your classroom? What resources does each have available—for example, does one have a computer available for homework and another does not?

2. *Process variables.* What resources, teaching systems, and specialist support are available?

3. *Output variables.* What does each student achieve as you apply processes to the students with their input realities? Are the data referenced to criteria (how well student has learned X), to norms (ranking or comparisons in a group), or to performance (accomplishment of a task)? Standardized tests are usually criterion-referenced or norm-referenced.

On the school district level, these categories get even broader. For example, inputs refer to teachers as well as to students. What certification and training does each teacher have? What is the teaching load of each teacher?

Educators should define the data variables that seem most relevant in their local system. The federal No Child Left Behind Act also requires disaggregation of data. This means sorting data on different groups (learning disabled, minorities, and so on) and on different strands to find answers to questions such as:

1. Are certain groups achieving less than others (that is, being left behind), and, if so, what can be done to remedy this?

2. Is the curriculum (content, processes, resources) failing to help students adequately master some specific learning strand, and, if so, what can be done to correct this?

As you view some of the data analyses in this section, watch for examples of addressing such questions.

Try this exercise. In the blank before each numbered item below, place the first letter of the type of data it represents, using "I" for input, "P" for process, and "O" for output data:

_____ 1. Teacher used multiple intelligence task options.

_____ 2. Student passed state mathematics test on the proficient level.

_____ 3. Student entered grade 9 reading on the sixth-grade level.

_____ 4. Teacher used rubric guides for students on all major task assignments.

_____ 5. Student tested low on a pretest on auditory discrimination.

Discuss your answers with a peer or with an instructor in a workshop on data management. What type of data is most useful to you?

Figure 33

Characteristics of Good Data

1. Relevant—measure what you wish to measure

2. Reliable—measure accurately

3. Timely—on time to be useful

4. Informative—clear and useful for diagnosis

5. Convenient—easily collected at the right level

Before looking at data analysis tools and examples of their use, let us examine one more page of background information in Figure 33. There are characteristics of good data that we need to pursue:

1. *Relevant.* What use are you going to make of the data? If you cannot answer that question, do not bother collecting them! Then, do the data you plan to collect provide you with the information needed for your planned use?

2. *Reliable.* Are the measurements accurate and comparable? For example, if you are comparing test data from different years, are you using the same standardized and validated test across those years? If not, different tests are apt to provide data that are not comparable and on which you cannot form valid conclusions.

3. *Timely.* Getting data that is useful for scheduling students into the right types of classes should come before the scheduling, not months after the students have been enrolled in the classes! This time gap is especially apt to happen if your source of data is state tests. For example, in the author's high school, results from the eighth-grade state mathematics test were never received until well after students started their grade 9 classes. In a regional school where we received high-school students from over 23 different K–8 districts, we had to administer our own entrance tests prior to fall classes in order to ensure a proper match between a student's prior learning and assigned mathematics classes.

4. *Informative.* Data have to be configured and exhibited in ways that make them easy to use. With few exceptions, raw data tables do not meet this standard. Certain types of charts and diagrams can help make data much easier to use.

5. *Convenient.* For the most part, elementary and secondary teachers face very demanding schedules. Carefully designed district plans should be implemented to ensure that:
   a. State, district, and schoolwide data are collected and reconfigured by others for convenient use by teachers.
   b. Technology support such as electronic gradebook software is made available with training to help teachers gather, reconfigure, and use data in individual classrooms without hours of extra work.

Comments are provided on some of these characteristics as we review specific tools and analyses in the remaining pages of this guide.

As we move to specific tools for the analysis of data, keep in mind this now common statement on quality management:

In God we trust, all others must bring data.[3]

This and similar statements are the foundation for accountability in public schools as well as in the business world today. More important, data help in the pursuit of mastery.

---

3. Jay Arthur, *The Small Business Guerrilla Guide to Six Sigma* (Denver, CO: LifeStar Publishing, 2004), p. 13.

Figure 2

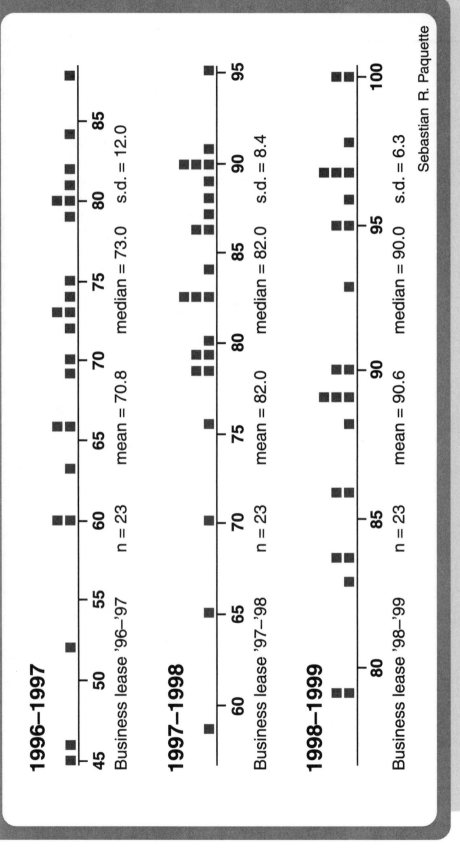

Do you remember Figure 2 comparing class grades from an electronic grade-book on an assignment across three years? This figure is shown again on page 72. Each black square represents the grade earned by one student. So we really have three sets of column graphs on the page. *Class grades with associated statistical analysis are an excellent way to determine whether new teaching techniques are leading to improved student performance on some major task.* In this case, new brain-compatible teaching methods introduced across two years did lead to improved performance.

You should consider two major points with this example:

1. Using electronic gradebooks can be an excellent way to make statistical analysis easy for teachers. In this case, the software did all of the statistical calculations and produced the visual displays that helped define a conclusion that the new teaching methods worked. See the resource section for more information on such software.
2. It is important to use some measure of central tendency and a standard deviation or spread calculation when making comparisons on grades.

Be sure you understand the central tendency and spread calculations.

Consider this sample set of grades and three different measures of central tendency:

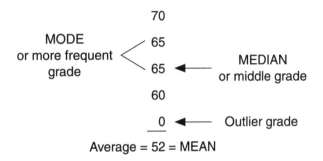

Quite often, grades that are far outside the majority pattern for a group or class of students affect the mean in a way that makes it an inaccurate figure to use to characterize class performance. When you are trying to make important conclusions about class performance or determine the impact of new instructional techniques, it can be important to use the median as your measure of central tendency in case outliers are distorting the mean (which, by the way, is not the case in Figure 2).

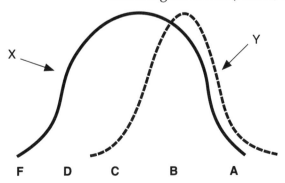

Finally, a standard deviation, or spread calculation, can add an important dimension to your analysis. You can refer to a book listed in the resource section for more information on standard deviation. For our purposes, simply be aware that in the following diagram of two grade distributions, curve Y has a smaller spread (width) than curve X. This is good because it means that fewer students are falling farther away from the higher grade area than in curve X.

Figure 34

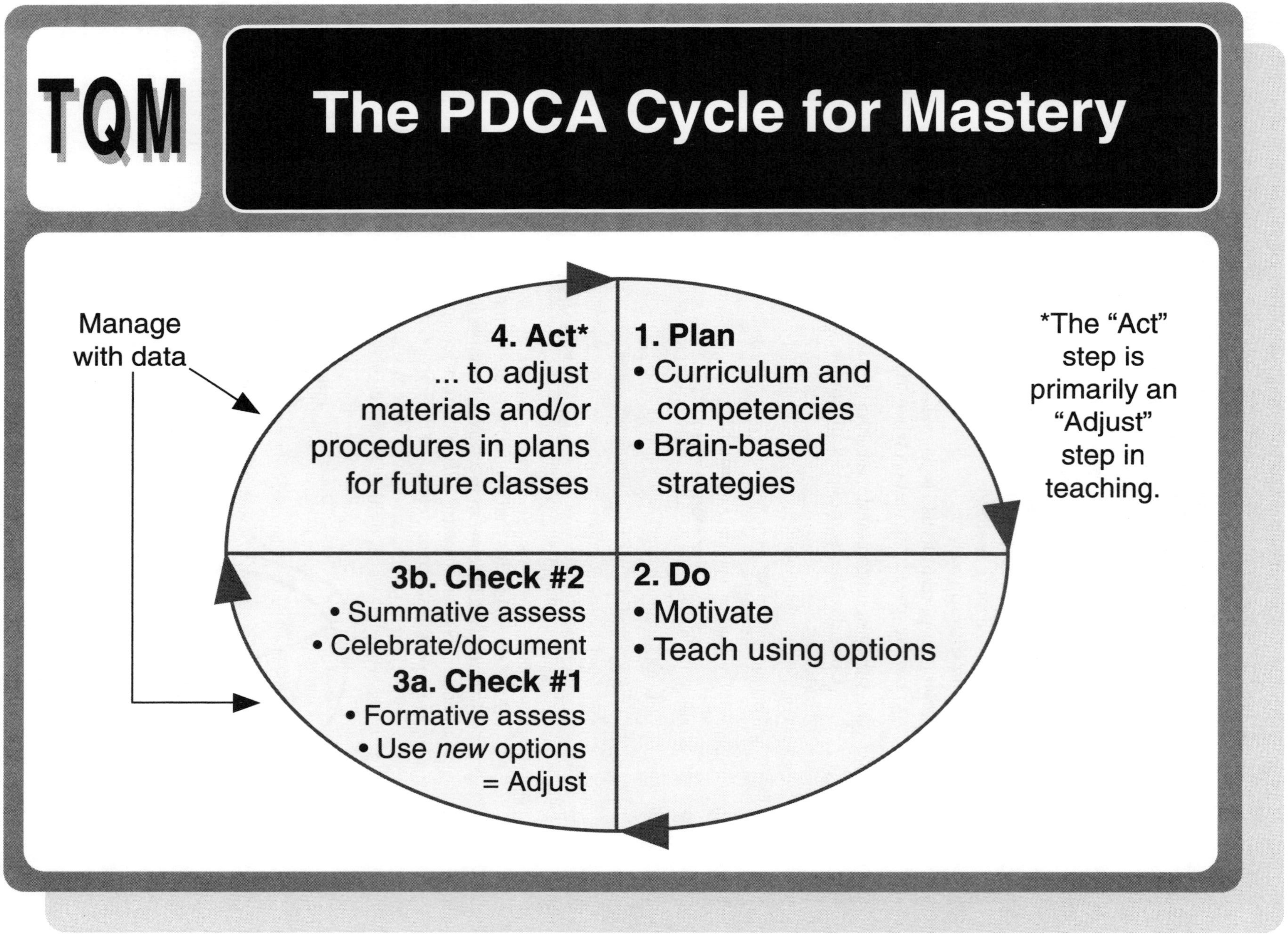

The PDCA Cycle for Mastery

TQM

*The "Act" step is primarily an "Adjust" step in teaching.

1. Plan
• Curriculum and competencies
• Brain-based strategies

2. Do
• Motivate
• Teach using options

4. Act*
... to adjust materials and/or procedures in plans for future classes

3b. Check #2
• Summative assess
• Celebrate/document

3a. Check #1
• Formative assess
• Use *new* options = Adjust

Manage with data

Let us look at a summary of the mastery approach, or Plan → Do → Check → Act/Adjust cycle, before we move to Section B-7 on specific tools for analysis. Follow the description in Figure 34.

The Plan and Do components of the cycle were covered in previous sections. In this mastery section, we have introduced the Check component of the cycle. The two types of checking are really processes that promote mastery. They are not a separate component, even though they are named and numbered separately from mastery in the summary figures presented near the beginning of this guide. So now we are describing the checking processes and mastery together.

Also be aware that checking and adjusting get mixed together. *We gather and check and analyze data in order to act on adjusting teaching techniques to achieve higher levels of mastery.*

It is important to recognize the two different phases of checking/adjusting that are necessary in an educational setting:

1. First, we check the performance of individual students—not to give them a grade, but to see if it is necessary to reteach or adjust instruction if some have not yet mastered a particular skill or competency. This is called formative or prescriptive assessment. This is not just a matter of determining competence. Rather, *this is where analysis comes into play*. We must work with some individual students to try to determine why they did not achieve and what might be the best way to correct the situation. Then we adjust or implement new learning options. This is step 3a in Figure 34.

2. Second, after reteaching, we can assess or test to give grades. This is called summative or documenting assessment. Here we determine both individual and class performance and use that data to work or analyze with students to define ways in which the teaching and reteaching procedures can be improved in the future. We also place documentation of learning into portfolios and/or other formats so that subsequent teachers will know where to start with each student. More comments are presented on this in Section B-8.

After all checking and analyzing is complete, the last step in the cycle is to Act to adjust teaching plans for future classes. For example, if many of the students had trouble achieving a certain competency in a learning unit, the teaching plan for that competency should be changed and strengthened before the unit is presented to a new class.

Since the Plan → Do → Check → Act/Adjust cycle is repeated indefinitely, it forms the basis for continuous improvement in teaching and learning. This cycle is the difference between the teacher who presents the same unit in the same way for 30 years and the teacher whose effectiveness keeps getting better and better on every unit he or she presents and manages. Teaching is a complex process. It is more difficult than many other professions. The great teachers are those who consciously and regularly address the joyful challenge of managing continuous improvement in the teaching and learning processes as they constantly deal with changing "raw materials" (students). Management of learning need never get boring; it is not a static process!

Figure 35

TQM

Basic Tools for Data Analysis

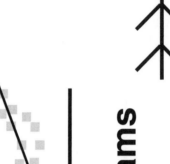

1. Column or bar charts

2. Pareto charts

3. Run charts

4. Scatter charts

5. Rubrics

6. Cause-and-effect diagrams

B-7. Checking and Adjusting

There are six simple checking tools listed in Figure 35. These tools will be adequate for solving 85 percent of the data-based analysis opportunities and problems faced by classroom teachers. More advanced tools can be useful at the district, specialist, or state levels.

While this section of the book will review some fundamentals, every teacher and administrator should pursue the goal of gaining a good conceptual background in the field of statistical analysis. An excellent self-study text for gaining this background is *Statistics Made Simple for School Leaders*,[4] published in partnership with the American Association of School Administrators.

Remember that the purpose of visual data displays is to facilitate the analysis of facts far more scientifically than can be done with intuition and common sense. Here is a brief summary of some ways to use each basic tool in the Check phase:

1. *Column or bar charts.* Use these charts to compare quantitative data on different groups or different categories. For example, test scores of separated or disaggregated groups are often compared this way on state assessment tests under the No Child Left Behind Act. Also, you can use bar charts to compare changes in average or individual achievement between different time periods, as we did in our English for the Entrepreneur example.

2. *Pareto charts.* Use Pareto charts to identify priorities to be addressed in a process. For example, with surveys and student help, you can identify what one or two changes in your teaching process would gain you the most positive reaction from your students.

3. *Run charts.* These allow you to visualize changes in data over a period of time. Such changes can be useful in measuring the effect of variation in teaching techniques.

4. *Scatter charts.* Scatter charts are used to determine whether or not a relationship exists between two factors. For example, does successful completion of homework assignments lead to correspondingly higher scores on the final examination in a course?

5. *Rubrics.* Published performance standards for specific assignments or types of assignments can help students monitor the quality of their work and can be used by teachers to determine where new instruction is needed.

6. *Cause-and-effect diagrams.* These diagrams are used to chart factors or actions that might contribute to an improved process or result. For example, if low reading scores are identified as contributing to low state assessment scores, you could chart the actions that you (or a brainstorming group) believe would lead to improved reading skills. These diagrams are often used in conjunction with the other tools listed above.

---

4. Susan Rovezzi Carroll and David J. Carroll, *Statistics Made Simple for School Leaders* (Lanham, MD, and Oxford: The Scarecrow Press, 2002).

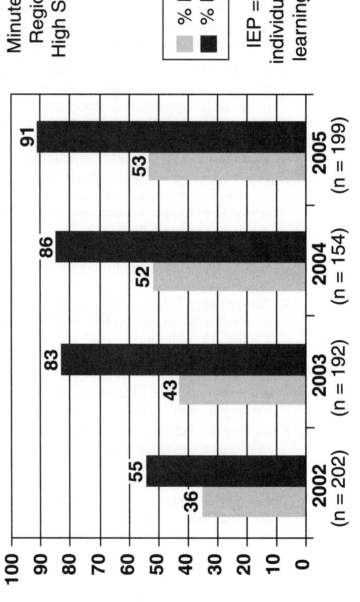

Figure 36

We begin a review of samples of these tools with the column chart. Refer to the column chart in Figure 36. The dark columns show the percentage of tenth graders passing the state language arts assessment test (MCAS) in a vocational high school on their first try. The high school was pursuing a multifactor plan to increase the passing percentage across the years shown. The dark columns indicate that the plan was promoting positive improvement in the passing percentage. However, that is only part of the story. The lighter columns show the percentage of students taking the test who had individualized education plans because of learning disabilities when they entered grade 9 in this grade 9–12 stand-alone high-school district. Despite a 47 percent increase in the number of entering students with learning disabilities in three years, the students and staff achieved a 65 percent increase in the number of students passing the state test after one year in the high school! Clearly, this staff deserved special recognition for promoting strong continuous improvement in student achievement. They were serving more than 3.5 times the percentage of allegedly learning-disabled students who were served in area non-vocational high schools.

Consider the false message that gets generated if absolute scores are not analyzed properly by looking at other factors:

The False Message	
1. Vocational-technical high schools are not promoting adequate academic achievement, as evidenced by *absolute scores* on state tests often being lower in vocational high schools than in non-vocational high schools.	2. Vocational-technical schools should increase their academic focus. *Translation*: They should concentrate on traditional academic classes and college preparatory programs.
The Accurate Data-Based Message	
1. Many vocational-technical high schools promote more *academic growth* than experiential* learners can achieve in traditional school environments. The lower state test scores that some students exhibit after one year in such schools are primarily the result of their K–8 non-experiential learning environments.	2. Highly linear, textbook-focused programs and unanalyzed state test results are failing to promote the achievement potential of thousands of students. *All* schools must give more attention to different learning styles. Federal and state leaders and media representatives should move beyond superficial absolute scores to analyzed growth statistics.

* Experiential learners are students who are more random than linear and who prefer concrete learning tasks focused on real-life problems. Unless given the proper learning task opportunities, they tend to fall behind in a highly linear, grade-specific curriculum. Then they may be labeled "learning disabled" or "special needs" students, even though they are just as capable as traditional learners who do well with abstract tasks in a linear curriculum.

In 2004, many national reports and No Child Left Behind test comparisons tended to focus on unexamined absolute scores rather than on growth scores and the need for more attention to different learning styles. This highlights a massive and destructive weakness in national policy.

Figure 37

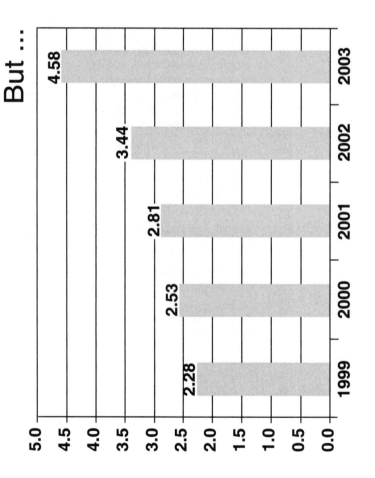

Reading Lab: Grade Equivalent Gain by Freshmen

TQM

But ...

Minuteman Regional High School

Let us review one more column chart to highlight some fundamentals of the use of such charts. Incidentally, if you turn the chart 90° so that the columns extend horizontally rather than vertically, the column chart becomes a bar chart. Some authors use the term "bar" to describe both orientations.

Figure 37 displays the average grade equivalent gain by year in a computerized reading lab for ninth graders. All freshmen who scored two or more years below grade level on a standardized reading test were assigned to this lab. They were taught to select programs matched to their learning style (visual or auditory) and to proceed at individual learning rates. You will see later why a particular software program was selected and supplemented with other actions to promote reading skills. For now, be aware of these realities:

1. Again, the data show constant improvement in program effectiveness. Components of the lab program are fine-tuned annually to continue this progress.

2. The word *but* associated with the 2003 column is a caution about the data. The standardized test used to measure student progress was the same from 1999 to 2002, but a new and not fully equivalent test was used in 2003. So a new data series will be started with 2003 data to ensure valid annual comparisons.

3. The fundamentals of the column chart remain the same:
   a. Categories (years, in this case) are on the horizontal axis.
   b. Results are on the vertical axis.
   c. A careful title and labels are applied, including where (the school) and when (the years) the data were collected.
   d. Normally the number (*n*) of students evaluated is recorded, as in Figure 36. That information was not included in this reading data, but it would have given readers an accurate concept of scale of measurement.
   e. The columns are separated and equally distant from each other, which is done automatically by the charting program (Excel, or PowerPoint's graph program, for most examples in this guide).

While it is possible to draw charts by hand with the help of grid-lined paper, electronic gradebooks and spreadsheet programs with charting capabilities make the classroom teacher's task easier in this area.

Spend some time thinking about ways in which you might use column charts to analyze data that would disclose useful numerical trends about aspects of your teaching. For example, one way in which many teachers use column charts is displaying the number of A, B, C, D, and F grades earned annually in a course or on a particular assignment. Then they analyze the reasons for the grades with students in order to identify actions that might improve future achievement. Subsequent charting will show whether improvement plans are working.

Figure 38

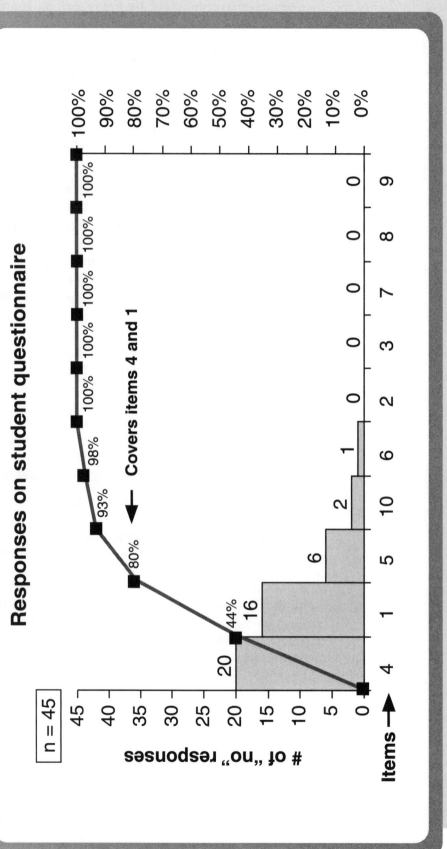

There are other variations of column charts. For example, histograms place value ranges from smallest to highest on the horizontal axis and the number of occurrences (or student scores) on the vertical axis. Column widths are arranged to abut each other, so the abutting columns tend to show a distribution curve.

One of the most useful variations is the *Pareto chart*. Refer to the example in Figure 38. The columns were used to plot the number of "no" responses to the first 10 statements on the Student Questionnaire shown on pages 84 and 85. The Pareto tool, in this case a subprogram of macro commands running in Excel, automatically plots columns from the highest occurrence first (20 "no" responses to question 4) to the lowest response. Therefore, in this case, the question provided the teacher with the visual message that if he addresses items 4 and 1, he will be addressing 80 percent of student evaluation concerns! The line chart above the columns and the horizontal scale on the right-hand side of the figure are automatically constructed by the Excel macro program from the LifeStar company listed in the resource section. That line chart gives the percentage of problems you will be addressing as you move from the left vertical axis across each column.

The usual way in which teachers use this research-based questionnaire is:

1. A teacher exchanges classes with a peer in the fall. Each administers and tabulates the questionnaires for the other, since students are more inhibited with their own teacher. Teachers need not share the results with administrators or evaluators.

2. Each teacher then develops and implements a plan to address the top two concerns of his or her students—that is, the two items that garnered the most "no" responses.

3. In the spring, the questionnaire is administered and tabulated again by the peer team. The results show whether students have seen improvement on the selected items.

4. The process is repeated annually, always addressing the two items on which the most students list concerns. It is a continuous improvement process in which students enjoy participating, especially if you have taught them principles of continuous improvement or quality management (more on that later). Administrators do not evaluate tabulated results, but teachers are expected to use the process.

Can you think of other ways to use Pareto analysis? What about improved or changed instruction on the two state test items answered incorrectly by the largest number of students? What about new behavior modification plans on the two types of discipline incidents that occur more often than any other types? Pareto analysis and follow-up give us a powerful process.

Incidentally, in the high school where we evolved this brain-based questionnaire that you are free to use, item 4 often scored as a high "no" item with newer teachers in their first year or two. Once the staff evaluation and in-service training programs made clear the motivation value of hooking or connecting students at the beginning of each unit, "no" responses on question 4 became less common, and teachers proudly insisted on sharing that fact. If you wish to use the questionnaire on the intermediate or secondary level, just white-out the page numbers and duplicate it as a two-sided document. A simpler questionnaire or oral questions would be necessary for lower grade levels.

Check one: _____ **Oct./Nov.** _____ **April/May**

Student Questionnaire

DIRECTIONS: Please give us your special help as we work to improve our learning service to you. At least twice per school year, give us your confidential (no names please) answer to each question on this form. Results will be summarized and used to improve future classes. Thanks.

Just check *one* column (either "Yes" or "No") after each of the first 10 items. If you check "No" on an item, try to write a suggestion for improvement in the space provided for that item. Finally, write separate answers to questions 11 and 12.

If more than one teacher serves the class, just give one rating to the teacher team.

	Usually:	
	Yes	No
1. The teacher gets to know me, my interests, and how I learn best. COMMENT/SUGGESTION:		
2. The teacher makes the classroom or lab a safe place where no one is harassed or embarrassed. COMMENT/SUGGESTION:		
3. The teacher maintains a firm, but friendly and fair environment. COMMENT/SUGGESTION:		
4. The teacher starts each unit in an interesting way. COMMENT/SUGGESTION:		
5. The teacher shows us how what is being taught can be useful in the real world. COMMENT/SUGGESTION:		

(continued)

(continued)

	Usually:	
	Yes	**No**
6. The teacher discovers when I need help and gives it to me. COMMENT/SUGGESTION:		
7. Class time is used efficiently for lots of learning. COMMENT/SUGGESTION:		
8. This class makes me plan and think about important things. COMMENT/SUGGESTION:		
9. I can see that my work is improving regularly. COMMENT/SUGGESTION:		
10. I like the learning materials and activities used (books, software, equipment, films, tasks, etc.). COMMENT/SUGGESTION:		
11. What do you like most about the class?		
12. What do you like least about the class?		

Again, thanks for your partnership help.

Figure 39

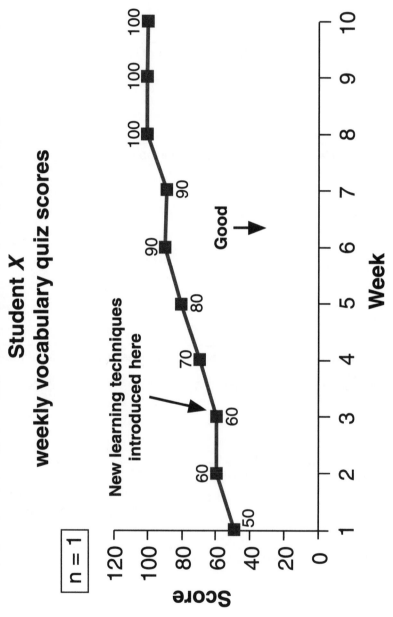

Run Chart: Student X Scores on Weekly Vocabulary Quiz

TQM

Consider Figure 39. This simple *run chart* is a record of one student's scores on a weekly vocabulary quiz. It is a fictitious example that illustrates several powerful practices used successfully in many schools. The practices are:

1. *Use of a weekly quiz.* This is an excellent practice for many grade levels and subjects. It helps to provide regular check points for both students and teachers in monitoring learning and identifying problems early. It can be formative (not for a grade) or summative (for a grade).

2. *Providing a visual picture of progress.* In Minuteman High School, a time-based chart like this has proven very valuable in parent-student-teacher conferences. The chart makes it easy to discuss trends, specific successes and problems, and the reasons for these with everyone focused on the same time and progress picture. For example, one rule of thumb in the field of statistical analysis is that data heading six or seven points in one direction—either higher or lower—is considered a strong trend. If the trend is better performance, success tends to motivate toward more success. If the trend is lower performance, it is time for intervention or change.

3. *Providing the context for useful messages.* There are two examples of this. First, the QI Macros software, described in greater detail on page 125, automatically generated and placed the "Good" comment and arrow on the chart. After three successive upward scores, the program is presenting motivating encouragement! Second, the teacher has placed an important record for analysis on the chart: the words "New learning techniques introduced here."

4. *Watching for the impact of new teaching or learning techniques.* If a record of the time at which any new techniques were introduced is placed on a run chart, the first clue as to whether or not those techniques are improving learning can be discovered. In this example, the teacher might be presenting weekly vocabulary lessons in an elementary school or more advanced word meanings in an SAT-preparation course in a high school. In either case, introducing visual context (pictures) to the learning task, using songs or rhythm, and using learning games all have strong potential for improving learning much more than do simple and often boring drill techniques. When you do introduce multiple learning styles and talent tasks, it is useful to discover their impact on learning.

The charting of weekly quiz scores for individual students and for the class average can be a very powerful process in encouraging learning improvement. This is especially true if quizzes are carefully designed to be highly relevant to defined course objectives. We shall discuss more on relevancy in the section on scatter charts.

Incidentally, there is no need to limit run charts to quiz scores or to something as narrow as the vocabulary example. General-knowledge quiz scores, or even weekly performance activity scores against rubric standards, can be used with good run chart practices.

A final suggestion on run charts is this: Require each student to maintain his or her own chart in middle schools and high schools. If you define a weekly system using standard scoring, you can print a chart outline on grid paper. The student will learn to monitor personal progress and develop an understanding of the concept of continuous improvement.

Figure 40

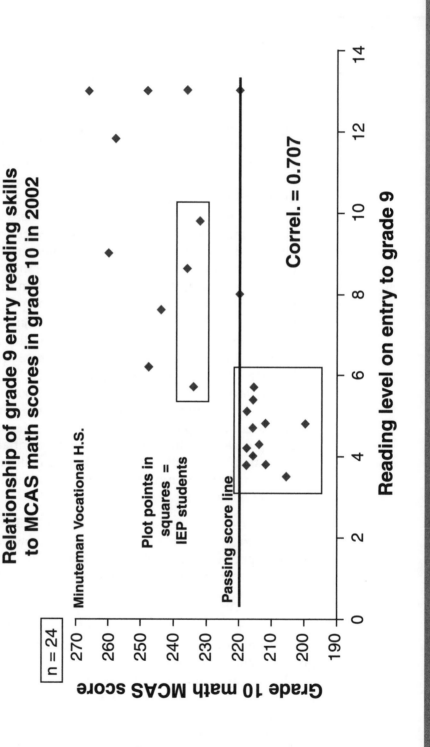

Scatter Chart Example: Exploring Relationships

TQM

Relationship of grade 9 entry reading skills to MCAS math scores in grade 10 in 2002

Minuteman Vocational H.S.

Plot points in squares = IEP students

Passing score line

n = 24

Grade 10 math MCAS score

Correl. = 0.707

Reading level on entry to grade 9

Review the *scatter chart* shown in Figure 40. Scatter charts are used to plot two sets of factors associated with some person (a student, for example), process, or occurrence. The usual purpose is to determine whether the two factors are related in some way. If you theorize that one factor is contributing to the other factor, that so-called causal factor is usually placed on the horizontal axis, and the suspected effect factor is placed on the vertical axis.

In this example, we selected the first 24 students from a class alphabetically and plotted their individual grade 9 entry-level grade-equivalent reading scores on a standardized test (Metropolitan Achievement Test) against their individual grade 10 scores on the Massachusetts MCAS mathematics test. Scores below 220 on the mathematics test were considered failing by the state. We also checked to see if each student had an individualized education plan (IEP) indicating the need for special services when he or she entered the school. In the chart, a square has been placed around the students who entered with IEPs. Excel, the program used, can also calculate the correlation coefficient, or strength of relationship between the two factors plotted. A correlation of +1 indicates a direct relationship; a correlation of 0 indicates no consistent relationship. If a correlation is negative, it means that when one factor increases, the other decreases. Three conclusions emerge from this chart:

1. In this sample, each student who failed the MCAS mathematics test on his or her first try in grade 10 had entered grade 9 reading below the sixth-grade level. However, one member of the sample who was reading below the sixth-grade level did pass the test.

2. In this sample, every student who failed the test had been judged in need of special services by his or her sending (K–8) school district. The sending schools and Minuteman are not in the same school district. Three students with individualized plans did pass the test.

3. The positive correlation between the two plotted factors is moderately high, 0.707. Thus, according to this sample, if a student enters grade 9 with reading skills below the sixth-grade level, he or she is part of a group in which approximately 50 percent of the MCAS math test result is related to the reading factor. Are you wondering where the 50 percent came from? Consider this table:

Judging Correlation Coefficients

+ or – Correlation Coefficient*	Strength of Correlation
0 to .30	None to low
.31 to .50	Low to moderate
.51 to .70	Moderate to high
.71 to .99	Strong

* To change the correlation coefficient to percentage of effect possibly related to the potential causing factor:
    1. Square the correlation coefficient
    2. Multiply the square by 100

In this example, can you see why the staff of Minuteman High School decided to focus strongly on improving the reading skills of certain incoming students? The school initiated a mandatory lab program and other activities for any student entering grade 9 with a grade-equivalent reading score below grade 6. We continue to explore this on the next page.

Figure 41

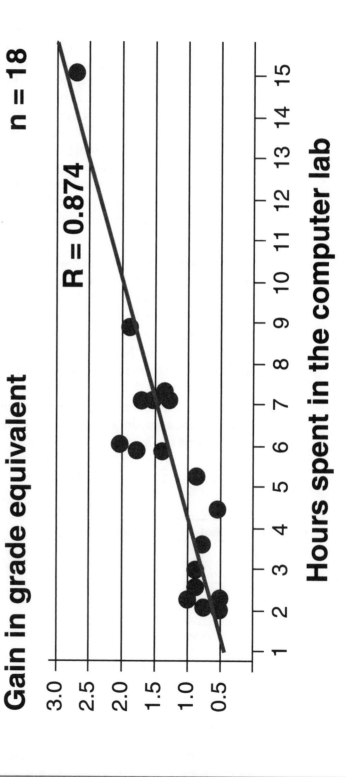

As you might guess, the data shown in Figure 40 led to extensive analysis and planning in the involved high school. A similar correlation between entry reading levels and initial scores on the state language arts test was identified. That correlation coefficient was 0.723. When an outside official suggested that perhaps the "fault" rested with vocational schools because some students who had passed the state MCAS mathematics test in grade 8 failed the tenth-grade version of the test on the first try, the Minuteman staff analyzed another set of factors. They plotted the grade 8 MCAS mathematics scores of students who failed the tenth-grade MCAS test against their tenth-grade scores. The correlation was 0.313. This is a low 9.8 percent relationship. In other words, passing the grade 8 test is not a good prediction of passing the grade 10 test, apparently because the test emphasis moves from arithmetic to more complex word problems. Word problems are difficult if you do not have adequate reading skills! Any high school that dares to help a significant percentage of lower-achieving students should be prepared to show the destructive fallacy in the unanalyzed use of absolute test scores that is common under federal and state education laws, at least in 2004. The criticisms directed at vocational-technical high schools in this regard are highly uninformed at best.

More important, all schools should use analyzed data to understand relationships and plan improvement. Figure 41 shows a scatter chart used for improvement planning in reading. You should try to have at least 24 students or other study objects in a scatter sampling in order to reduce distortion by any outlier data. However, smaller samplings can be useful indicators of relationships. The Minuteman staff began identifying factors that would help the school provide very effective growth in reading skills to any students needing that help on the high-school level. After visiting many schools and reviewing numerous products, they decided to test a reading-improvement software program that allowed students to select different styles and rates of learning. The scatter chart in Figure 41 shows the results of that testing: a 0.874 correlation coefficient, a very strong relationship between time spent in the lab and gain in reading skill. The school purchased this powerful program and hundreds of students have benefited.

What uses can you and your students find for identifying important relationships? For example, is there a strong relationship between completion of homework assignments and course grades earned in your class? Is there a relationship between attendance and grades? Do high weekly test scores lead to high final examination scores? The answers to such questions are not always what you would expect. For example, one teacher found very little correlation between attendance at weekly help sessions he offered and improved examination scores. In working with him to discover the reason, the staff found that in the help sessions he was emphasizing parts of the curriculum that were not in the final examination; he changed that.

Do not view one chart analysis as presenting *the* answer to an improvement problem. In the reading case, the staff designed multiple activities in a coordinated system. You will see this when we cover cause-and-effect diagrams because we selected that critical area to highlight the theme that was introduced at the beginning of this guide—the system approach.

Here are two final comments on the scatter chart. Be sure to calculate the correlation coefficient. It is more objective than the chart alone, which could get distorted by size or scale decisions related to display. Also, add a trend line, as shown in Figure 41, for more visual clarity; in this case, the QI Macros program for Excel added the line automatically.

Figure 42

TQM

Sample Rubric for a Paragraph

_1_ 1. Has a clear topic sentence

_2_ 2. Has (3) supporting sentences

_3_ 3. Has transition sentences as needed

_4_ 4. Has a "clincher" sentence

_5_ 5. Has clarity of focus

_6_ 6. Has good word choice and tone

_7_ 7. Has correct grammar, capitalization, punctuation, and spelling

Adapted from Minuteman H.S.

Rubrics are one of the most powerful assessment and measurement tools that a teacher can use. Examine the sample rubric in Figure 42. It was adapted from one used in a basic high-school English class. One can debate or clarify the criteria; for example, the number of supporting sentences could certainly vary. However, a rubric exhibits these characteristics:

1. It is skill-oriented, and each skill can be taught. Therefore, it is useful across many assignments, not just for one task.
2. Each skill can be measured. For example, irrelevant sentences would detract from "focus." Offensive or incorrectly used words would detract from "good word choice and tone."
3. Students can use the criteria to judge their own work.
4. The teacher can measure how an individual or the entire class is performing on each and every skill.

Does this last point lead you to imagining the management power inherent in rubric measurement?

Assume that you are evaluating a paragraph constructed by each of 20 students in your class. For each criterion item, you record the number of students *not* meeting the criterion. You place the results in an Excel spreadsheet in this form:

Criterion Item	Number of Students Not Meeting the Criterion
1	1
2	3
3	7
4	11
5	8
6	6
7	4

(n = 40 negative evaluations)

The spreadsheet contains the subprogram QI Macros. So you simply select the two columns of data, go to the QI Macros menu, and select "Pareto Chart." The chart below automatically appears. It clearly shows that you can address 48 percent of the problems by improving instruction on "clincher" sentences (criterion item 4) and clarity of focus (item 5). Data from a rubric can focus your instructional improvement efforts.

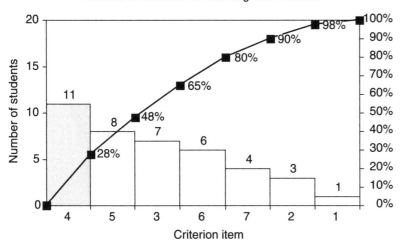

Number of students not meeting each criterion

Figure 43

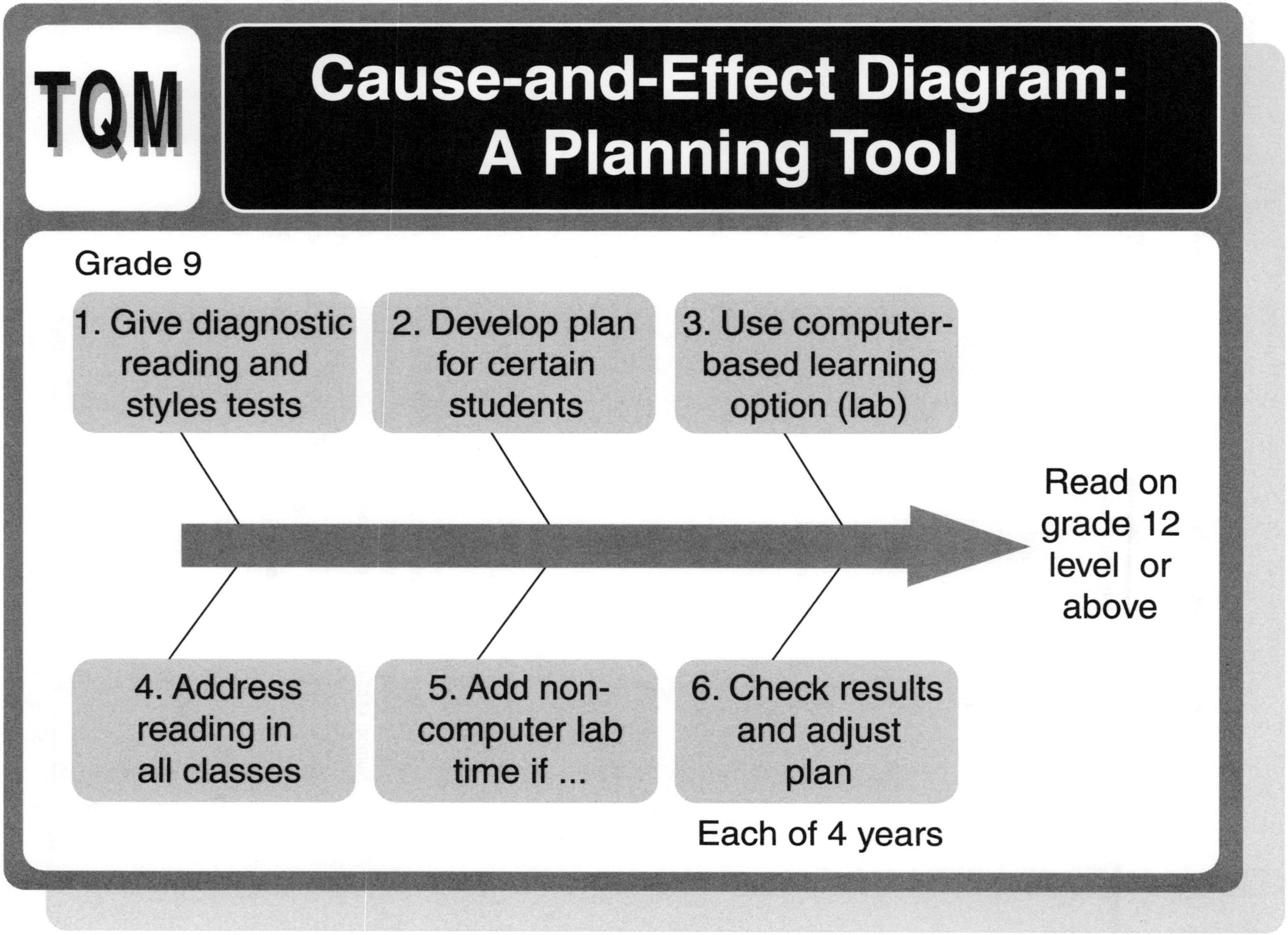

TQM

Cause-and-Effect Diagram: A Planning Tool

Grade 9

1. Give diagnostic reading and styles tests

2. Develop plan for certain students

3. Use computer-based learning option (lab)

4. Address reading in all classes

5. Add non-computer lab time if ....

6. Check results and adjust plan

Read on grade 12 level or above

Each of 4 years

Previously, we described a high-school situation in which a significant number of students reading below grade level were accepted for grade 9 entry. The staff analyzed the reading data and discovered that these students had great difficulty using their technical lab textbooks. This led to the staff using a *cause-and-effect diagram*, a basic tool for developing a plan to improve any situation.

Figure 43 shows an action plan developed by a staff team at Minuteman Regional High School. This type of plan is essentially a list of actions or causes that you believe are leading or will lead toward a certain result or goal. This is the concept:

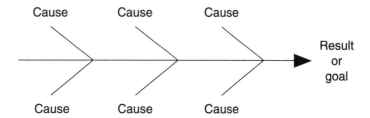

In this case, the desired goal was to have each student reach the twelfth-grade level or above in reading skill before high-school graduation.

The elements of the plan are:

1. Give diagnostic tests on reading skills and styles of learning to each incoming student.
2. Develop an individual improvement plan for each student reading two or more grade levels below the grade 9 entry level.
3. Provide a new major resource to all selected students—for example, the computer-based lab with options for different learning styles and learning rates described on page 90.
4. Provide training and assistance to *all* teachers on promoting reading skills in *all* subjects (academic and vocational-technical).
5. Add other special help classes and options to individual plans for students with special needs and for students who do not seem to profit from the computer-based reading lab.
6. Annually monitor and adjust plans for each selected student.

This plan was developed even further after new data showed a strong relationship between reading levels on entering grade 9 and state assessment test scores in grade 10. The school added a special program for students needing help with auditory discrimination in order to improve reading ability. The evolving plan did not lead to immediate achievement of the stated goal. However, as shown in Figure 37 on page 80, it promoted major and continuous movement toward that goal. Quality is a direction, not an absolute.

Cause-and-effect diagrams are powerful visual thinking and planning tools. Most departments and teams at Minuteman High School use this tool very effectively with associated data. All students in the high school are also given training in the use of this and other quality management tools. In fact, in K–12 schools across the nation, students of all ages are using what some elementary students call the "sticky fish" diagram (because it looks like the skeleton of a fish). It helps students as well as teachers in developing planning abilities as they address complex tasks on the road to quality. Try it with your classes.

Figure 44

Spreadsheet Power:
Analyzing Test Results

TQM

MCAS language arts, 2004, Minuteman H.S.

Question no.	% Multiple choice incorrect	Learning strand no.	Learning strand description
29	62	13	**Nonfiction** Understand and identify irony
26	54	15	**Figurative language** Identify hyperbole
21	52	15	**Style and language** Identify mood of text
16	49	14	**Poetry** Identify figure of speech—Personification
35	48	5	**English structure** Identify parallel structure

Sort column

Spreadsheets and databases can be extremely useful tools for analyzing test results and other measurements. Figure 44 shows the first five rows of an Excel spreadsheet displaying data from a state test, sorted by the percentage of students answering each multiple-choice question incorrectly. Because the highest percentage of incorrect test answers is listed first, you can immediately identify the questions and learning strands on which the most students made errors. Because the state eventually publishes the questions and another report shows what answers students gave, you can determine whether your curriculum should be strengthened or changed or whether a specific question is simply confusing. The latter does happen. For example, many students answered a genre question incorrectly on the 2003 Massachusetts language arts test because the author of the essay wrote about personal experiences, leading many students to label the selection as biographical. Confusing questions aside, the sorted data provide you with the power to analyze data effectively.

Because the data shown are in an Excel spreadsheet, they can be easily sorted and converted to charts for visual clarity. If you prefer to have priorities for analysis shown in a Pareto chart, that can be done quickly with the QI Macros program described on page 83. However, once question data are sorted from highest number incorrect to lowest number incorrect, the priorities for analysis are clear in the spreadsheet without having to produce a Pareto chart. Minuteman High School departments immediately focus their analysis on any items and strands that at least 50 percent of students answer incorrectly.

Two special points should be considered on spreadsheets:

1. This is an area in which outside organizations and/or school specialists can be very helpful to teachers. In the example used, state results data were converted to useful database options in TestWiz:Massachusetts by a company called data-Metrics (paid by the state) and sorted in a Microsoft Access database by the high school's computer specialist, who then moved the data into different Excel files useful to different instructional departments.

2. With Excel and/or subprograms like QI Macros from LifeStar, individual teachers can access a broad range of statistical analysis procedures without buying commercial gradebook software. See the resource section for more information.

There is really no reason for any school to operate without the power of data analysis to improve instruction and learning. Here is a partial list of some important tools available in Excel and QI Macros for Excel:

Basic Charts in Excel	Added Capabilities from QI Macros
Column chart	Pareto chart
Bar chart	Histogram (easier than using Excel alone)
Line chart	Cause-and-effect diagram (a little awkward
Pie chart	with drawing)
Scatter (X,Y) chart	Control charts
	Note: Also gives access to the "correlation"and "rank and percentile" calculations available in Excel.

Again, see the resource section for more information.

Table of Sample Adjustments Based on Data Analysis

Tool Used	Sample Adjustments Made
Column chart	Compared percentage of students passing state tests from year to year to decide whether to continue or expand certain remedial programs. Programs were expanded.
	Compared average grade-level gain in reading skill from year to year in a computer-based lab program to determine whether annual adjustments in techniques were adding value to the program. Increasingly positive results led to stronger staffing support for that program.
Pareto chart	Used a chart of negative responses on a student questionnaire to develop an improvement plan for the techniques most criticized by students.
Run chart	Tracked weekly quiz scores to determine whether new teaching/learning techniques were associated with improved achievement. Refined techniques on the basis of the results.
Scatter chart	Compared entry-level reading scores with passing data from state tests to identify relationships. Led to identifying reading skill as a primary factor. New programs were created.
	Computed correlation between time spent in a reading lab and gain in reading skills to decide whether to purchase the expensive lab. Answer was "yes."
Rubric	Tabulated the number of students not meeting each rubric criterion in writing to determine which areas of teaching/learning most needed improvement. Lessons were modified.
Cause-and-effect diagram	Diagrammed the factors in an improvement plan and used that to guide separate investment and evaluation efforts.
Spreadsheet	Supported item analysis of state test results to determine where curriculum efforts might be most productive. Those items became the primary focus of improvement efforts.

Of course, checking with data has one major purpose—to identify areas and/or ways in which you can adjust instruction to continue supporting more improvement in student achievement. The Table of Sample Adjustments on page 98 provides a brief review of adjustments that were made with the simple tools described on pages 76–97.

Keep three major points in mind regarding the samples:

1. The samples are listed in the order in which they appear in the book, not in chronological sequence. For example, in reality, the cause-and-effect diagram to plan for reading improvement came before the column and scatter charts used to evaluate the effectiveness of a specific reading lab.
2. This book just scratches the surface on the many ways a teacher can use data to guide improvement efforts. It is simply intended to help any teacher start on that powerful path.
3. Data organization and analysis with tools is not a strictly sequential process. Data are used in planning, in checking, and in re-planning. Reflect on this statement for a while.

The best way for any teacher to begin using the power of managing learning with data is to study the principles and examples in this book *and* to attend a hands-on workshop that provides practice in this area.

Before continuing to the last component of Section B, the heart of the book, review the content:

B-1. The Planning Factor

B-2. Motivation Factors

B-3. Preparing Students

B-4. Providing Style Choices

B-5. Providing Learning Task or Talent Choices

B-6. Promoting Mastery with Data

B-7. Checking and Adjusting

B-8. Celebrating and Documenting

Any teacher who works diligently on strengthening these eight components in his or her classroom can move from:

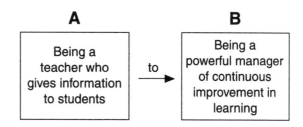

B is the proper professional level in best service to students.

Project Evaluation Sheet

1. NAME: _____ GRADE: __11__

2. PROJECT TITLE: _Environmental Glass Sorting Machine (EGSM)_

3. BRIEF DESCRIPTION: _Device separates glass containers on_ _the basis of optical discrimination of color differences._

4. COMMENTS ON COMPETENCIES APPLIED IN: _Electromechanics_

a. Gathering and processing information

b. Arranging resources

Completed research on: 1. An environmental problem 2. Optical sensing 3. Computer control 4. Programming   (copy available on request)

1. Developed the project
   plan and schedule
2. Acquired proper materials
   for simulation
3. Completed project on
   schedule

c. Selecting and using technology

d. Using a system (TQM) approach

1. Selected the right tools 2. Used troubleshooting to   eliminate problems

Applied quality control to system operation to reach a 100 percent success rate

e. Exercising interpersonal and/or leadership skills

1. Consulted with teachers and students 2. Prepared an associated marketing presentation   (available on request)

5. EVALUATOR COMMENTS on (date) _____3-8-93_____ : ___A+___

Met all quality control standards. Recommended for portfolio with pictures.

Signature: _____ Title: ___Teacher___

B-8. Celebrating and Documenting

There are two well-researched realities that make *celebrating and documenting* important activities in a system for teaching:

1. Students, like everyone else, are attracted to activities in which they have experienced success. Put simply, success encourages more success. Therefore, when students succeed, the success should be celebrated. The celebration is an important verification of learning that in turn encourages self-confidence and more learning.

2. Documentation, or records, on learning is important information for a student and his or her next teachers. For example, we can be most effective in improving reading skills if we know the student's skill level before we begin to seek improvement. Records also provide important information for parents and, in the case of high-school graduates, for college admissions officers and prospective employers.

Let us consider a powerful way to celebrate and document.

Page 100 shows an actual example of a project evaluation sheet that fulfilled both celebration and documentation functions at the high-school level. The school began using this type of form, which it called *portfolio sheets*, in 1993. This particular form was developed for culminating projects or tasks undertaken by students. The categories for competencies (a–e) were judged to be important to all projects or tasks. At the conclusion of the project shown on page 100, the teacher completed the form, gave a grade, and made recommendations. The completed form was given to the student and, along with a Polaroid picture of this eleventh-grade project, placed in his course notebook. Consider the value of this record:

1. Along with oral praise or congratulations from the teacher, the sheet gave a record of success that the student could proudly show to his parents. Of course, in this case he also demonstrated his successful project to the entire class and others including interested teachers and administrators. (It was a great project built with LEGO materials, by the way.)

2. Added to other notebook records, the project record gave the student's twelfth-grade teachers a good insight into his capabilities. They could also request a printout of the computer program and his written marketing presentation, mentioned on the project evaluation sheet.

3. Both college admissions officers and prospective employers could eventually be shown this and other portfolio materials.

Students have experienced some very positive reactions to portfolios or project records shown to both college officials and employers. A student in the English for the Entrepreneur course constructed a truly outstanding business plan, the major culminating project for the course. After graduation, he applied to a prestigious college with high SAT standards. His SAT score would normally have led to a rejection. However, when he showed his business plan project, with all of its computer-generated charts and analyses, in an admission interview, he was admitted and was even asked if the college could use his business plan as a model in its classes!

Figure 45

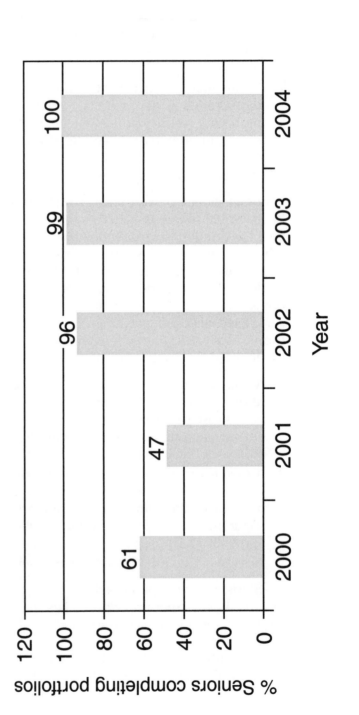

TQM

Growth of Portfolio System:
Minuteman High School

The use of project evaluation or portfolio sheets eventually proved so useful in many courses that the Minuteman staff decided to implement a practice of encouraging every course to join in the creation of a portfolio for every student in the 1999–2000 school year. This became a standard Plan → Do → Check → Act process. The chart in Figure 45 shows that the percentage of seniors completing portfolios decreased from 61 percent in June 2000 to 47 percent in June 2001. A staff task force worked with participation and quality data in the summer of 2001 and implemented major changes in the 2001–2002 school year, including full staff training, new quality standards, and a schoolwide "requirement." Participation then increased to 96 percent in 2002 and finally to 100 percent in June 2004, all with constantly measured and improving quality.

Many other school systems have implemented portfolio programs. We have seen portfolio boxes used effectively in elementary schools. We have seen optional systems, rigid systems, and flexible systems used at all grade levels. Each year, a staff task force measures participation in and quality of student portfolios and monitors developments in other school districts and/or in reported research. Then an improvement plan is prepared and implemented.

The celebration and documentation benefits of the portfolio process have become very clear to staff and students alike. A bonus benefit also developed under the No Child Left Behind Act. Our state started allowing special-needs students who did not quite reach the state pass score to have portfolios considered as alternative proof of learning on state curriculum standards. As this guide was being written, the high-school staff was again modifying the portfolio program in order to ensure that any student having state test problems is given a fair opportunity to demonstrate required learning through the portfolio structure.

Extensive details on Minuteman's specific portfolio program are not provided here because the program evolves annually. However, staff experience and observations of other districts have led to these general guidelines:

1. A celebrate and document program should be *required*. The purposes served are too valuable to be left to chance or the inclinations of individual staff or team members.

2. The program should be "grown," not mandated overnight. For example, in the first year or two, Minuteman teachers "played" with different approaches until staff and students became familiar with the values and procedures and identified practices that seemed effective and reasonable.

3. A staff task force should direct a Plan → Do → Check → Adjust process that includes the evaluation of quality and participation levels. That group should plan and implement staff training and the availability of mentors to assist any teacher or student encountering a problem.

4. The system should be evolved locally and in relation to grade levels. For example, the file box approach seems to work well for self-contained elementary classrooms, but it would not be practical in a high school with constant movement from classroom to classroom.

Figure 46

Sample Topics in a Grade 9–12 Student Curriculum on Managing Quality

- **Stories from the history of managing quality**
- **W. Edwards Deming's Profound Knowledge principles**
- **Characteristics of effective teaming (experiences)**
- **Use of basic tools for managing quality:**
  - Brainstorming
  - Force field analysis
  - Flowcharts
  - Cause-and-effect diagrams
  - Pie charts
  - Column/bar charts
  - Histograms
  - Pareto charts
  - Run charts
  - Scatter charts
  - Check sheets and surveys
  - Control charts
    - (in technical classes)
- **Application in personal learning and a career study area**

C. Students as Partners in Quality

In Section B-3 on preparing students, it was suggested that students be taught about style and talent preferences in order to help them learn how to learn. The same suggestion holds true for the principles of managing for quality.

If a student learns the powerful history of the quality movement and is given the opportunity to actually use tools for analyzing data, he or she gains two major advantages in our very competitive global economy:

1. He or she is better prepared to function in the many business and industry organizations that now use quality management principles and tools.
2. He or she has the best opportunity to apply principles of quality management both in school/college learning and in every aspect of personal and career development.

In this context, Figure 46 shows some topics in a student curriculum on managing quality for grades 9–12 at Minuteman Regional High School. This curriculum was carefully scheduled and coordinated so that even when a student changed courses, he or she would not miss any of the basic units.

The exact content of such a curriculum varies according to grade level. Outstanding materials and examples from schools across the nation are available from Koalaty Kid, the American Society for Quality's K–12 quality in education initiative. See the resource section for more information on Koalaty Kid. For now, simply be aware that many elementary schools have been leaders in this movement. More than 200 schools have had their staff teams trained in Koalaty Kid (elementary) or Quality Keys (sixth through twelfth grade) processes.

The ideal arrangement in a K–12 school district is to have students in every elementary and secondary school operating with quality principles. This offers strong support for No Child Left Behind progress because:

1. No Child Left Behind progress depends on the Plan → Do → Check → Act cycle of continuous improvement in quality.
2. A quality curriculum helps students understand and live the continuous improvement process. They become true partners in managing with data, not because of a law, but because it is the basis of global competition today.

Once students understand and participate in the improvement process, teachers' jobs become easier. The teacher-student team is more efficient than teachers and students operating in essentially separate roles.

While student materials are best developed on a grade-level basis, the TQM Guide entitled Total Quality Management in Education, on pages 106–109, can be used with adults as a four-page summary of quality management concepts in education. It can give teachers, administrators, school board members, and parents common ground for discussion when a teacher-student partnership for managing quality is proposed.

TQM Total Quality Management in Education
TQM Guide, Basic

The New Global Economy

Why Get Involved with TQM?

TQM is a philosophy and system for continuously improving services and/or products offered to customers. Now that the technologies of transportation and communication have replaced national economic systems with a global economy, nations and businesses that do not practice TQM can easily become "losers" in economic competition. The educational system of a nation is the basic tool for preparing citizens to be TQM practitioners. Therefore, the potential benefits of TQM in a school, district, or college are very clear:

1. TQM can help a school or college provide better service to its primary customers—students and employers.
2. The continuous improvement focus of TQM is a fundamental way of fulfilling the accountability requirements defined by No Child Left Behind legislation.
3. Operating a no-fear TQM system with a focus on continuous growth and improvement offers more excitement and challenge to students and teachers than does a "good-enough" learning environment. Therefore, the climate for learning is improved.

What Are the Essential Elements of TQM in Education?

In a TQM school or college, improvement teams and individuals are constantly working on improving service to customers. The concept of a service being "good enough" is considered inadequate. Thorough understanding of the differences between traditional and TQM schools is best developed in a dynamic seminar, not in a simple written guide; therefore, this guide is intended to supplement such a seminar. Each of the following elements is very important for fully realizing the potential of TQM in education:

1. Awareness and Commitment for Everyone

The linguistic, kinesthetic, visual, and/or mathematical talents of students will not be developed to their fullest potential unless *every* member of a teaching-learning partnership promotes the highest possible quality at each step in the development process. A transformation from "good-enough" or traditional education (where grades of "A" and "B" are good enough even if they do not represent the best work) should begin with everyone being made aware of the potential of TQM and its elements. An excellent way to begin is with a total staff meeting with parents and school board members participating. The meeting can provide:

- A dynamic overview of TQM elements and potential by one or more presenters who have experienced both
- A clear commitment from the school board, superintendent, and principal that they will fully support TQM efforts and that they do not expect (to use the language of W. Edwards Deming) "instant pudding" results

2. A Clear Mission

Managing continuous movement toward progressively higher quality standards depends on defining those standards. If a TQM steering committee is formed in a school (See item 10a), it should determine the answer to this question: Does the school have a clear, customer-focused mission statement and a functioning process for divisions and/or departments that translates this statement into exit outcomes for graduates? If the answer is "no," that problem must be addressed with local, state, national, and employer standards. These standards should emphasize developing students' abilities to solve real-life problems rather than just memorizing subject matter. The latter does not represent quality for either students or employers.

3. A Systems Planning Approach

Traditional education has become excessively compartmentalized. Teacher *X* provides an English course; science teacher *Y* might focus heavily on a student's knowledge of scientific principles without paying much attention to developing that student's ability to use English principles in writing a technical report. Subconsciously, the student begins to view English as a *course* instead of a skill to be *used*. If higher levels of student competence are to be developed, there must be higher levels of systemwide and cross-departmental *planning* for instructional improvement in schools and colleges. Lack of system planning is a serious obstruction to higher quality in student learning. Compare this schoolwide reading development plan in a middle school to what you know about narrower traditional remedial reading programs:

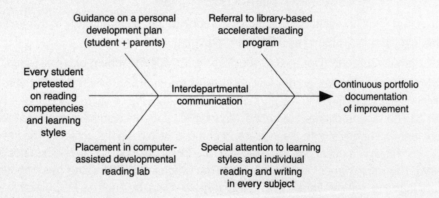

Of course, such a system approach to learning improvement normally happens only if interdepartmental planning arranges it.

4. Teaming Replacing Hierarchy

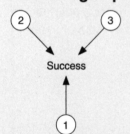

The hierarchical organizations of yesterday are still dominant in too many businesses and schools. Such organizations tend to promote individual effort that is good enough to satisfy a supervisor who sometimes knows less about how to achieve quality than those he or she supervises. Cross-departmental teams promote stronger improvement if they are:

- Given a clear mission and strong authority
- Supported rather than hampered by supervisors

Support is a major factor in the success of TQM. If administrators, supervisors, and department chairpersons support task improvement teams, those teams can generate more motivation and improvement than can otherwise be achieved. If not, TQM cannot achieve its potential. In properly operated TQM programs, administrators and supervisors work diligently at:

- Insisting on clear visions and missions
- Coordinating among task or improvement teams
- Supporting the efforts and authority of improvement teams to the highest possible degree

These are very critical support actions. If administrators and supervisors do not fulfill them properly, task improvement teams may fail.

5. Enablement AND Empowerment Replacing Fear

Training Pays Dividends

Traditional evaluation systems can generate fear and stifle initiative. Staff members focus on doing whatever keeps the boss happy. However, if volunteer members of *empowered* improvement teams are given opportunities to become experts and/or to use experts, that *enabling* generates excitement and dedication. School districts should support members of quality improvement teams with funding and time for conferences, seminars, visits to other schools, use of consultants, planning and sharing with others, and so on. Teams function best if team members are given the background and authority to make informed decisions. Each district and school should define and implement objectives for a strong focus on being a learning organization, an organization in which everyone is a learner on paths to quality improvement.

6. Focus on Mastery Learning

In traditional classrooms, teachers often follow this sequence:

Plan → Teach → Test

The normal curve that usually results stands as a testimony to the fact that many students fail to learn at the highest possible level in this system. The TQM alternative is:

1. Plan → 2. Teach (Do) → 3. Check** → 4. Revised teaching (Act) → 5. Test**

In the Check step, formative (not-for-grade) testing is used to determine which learning some students have missed. Then non-mastered material is retaught in some different way or style. If advisable, the checking and revised teaching can be repeated more than once. Meanwhile, students who have mastered the material move on to enrichment learning or assist with the instruction of those who have not achieved mastery. This system of mastery learning can result in much more complete learning for most students—in effect, a positive movement of the "normal" curve. This improvement in learning is a basic purpose of TQM in the classroom. For an excellent review of mastery learning, refer to *Implementing Mastery Learning*, by Thomas R. Guskey (1996), Wadsworth Publishing Company, Belmont, CA.

7. Management by Measurement

The previous section introduced an adapted Shewhart Cycle, a basic part of a TQM process. Be aware that measurement is very important in the ** marked steps of this cycle. For example, if a reading teacher used a new computer program in the Act step to assist students having trouble, he or she might gather data in steps 3 and 5 and plot them in a scatter chart to investigate the relationship between the use of that program and final learning results:

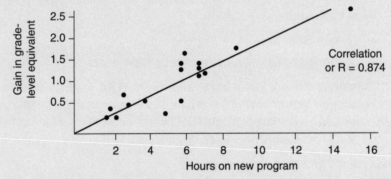

If careful analysis showed that the new program promoted strong progress in reading, that would affect planning for future instruction. This management by data rather than by opinion allows objective pursuit of the two basic purposes of TQM in education:

a. Improved learning
b. Improved cost-effectiveness

Excellent books on quality processes and measurement in education are available from a free catalog from ASQ Quality Press, P.O. Box 3005, Milwaukee, WI, 53201-3005. Call ASQ at 800-248-1946 or Fax at 414-272-1734. Member discounts are available to those who join the American Society for Quality. ASQ's Web site is http://www.asq.org. State or regional chapters also exist; for example, the Web site for the Boston chapter is http://www.asqboston.org.

8. Development of Student TQM Skills

In addition to using TQM to improve learning in general, every school district should specifically equip its students to understand and use TQM. This is a basic part of schools contributing to readiness for work in the global economy. Whether a school staff decides to integrate learning TQM into existing courses or to provide it as a separate course, it is important that students *do* TQM, not just study about it. Excellent resources in this area are:

a. Total Quality Curriculum, from Skills USA-VICA, Education Dept., P.O. Box 3000, Leesburg, VA, 20177-0300. Call 703-777-8810; Fax at 703-777-8999. This high-school curriculum was developed in a partnership between educators and quality leaders from industry. The Web site is http://www.skillsusa.org.

b. Selected books from ASQ Quality Press at the address shown in Section 7. These books are relevant to student activities: (1) *Thinking Tools for Kids* (Barbara A. Cleary and Sally J. Duncan, 1999); (2) *Future Force: Kids That Want to, Can, and Do!* (Elaine McClanahan and Carolyn Wicks, 1999); and (3) *Continuous Improvement in the Science Classroom* (Jeffery J. Burgard, 2000).

An excellent way to have students live TQM is to establish a system in which student assessment portfolios are dynamic records of constant improvement in which the students can take great pride.

9. A Humanistic and Brain-Compatible Focus in the Learning Environment

Dr. William Glasser has provided one of the best translations of TQM principles into suggestions for a very productive learning environment. Every educator can profit from reading his book, *The Quality School Teacher* (New York: HarperCollins, 1998). It provides information on six conditions for quality schoolwork:

a. There must be a warm, supportive learning environment.
b. Students should be asked to do only useful work.
c. Students should be asked to do the best they can do.
d. Students should be asked to evaluate their own work and improve it.
e. Quality work should always feel good.
f. Quality work should never be destructive.

It is important that educators consider Dr. Glasser's work and suggestions carefully. Working with people is much more complex than manufacturing widgets. Dr. Glasser offers an excellent blueprint for TQM in classrooms in the context of deep sensitivity to human relationships. One of the most productive areas in which a school task improvement team can work is in helping all staff members use more brain-compatible techniques in teaching. Most of what we know about how the brain works has been discovered in the last 15 years. Dr. Glasser's fine work is just one piece of information now available on improving the effectiveness of teaching.

10. A Transformation Plan

In Section 1, an awareness presentation was recommended as the first step in considering transformation from traditional to TQM operation. Two other basic actions are recommended here:

a. Form a TQM steering committee that:

• Develops a plan for $\longrightarrow\!\!\!\longrightarrow\!\!\!\longrightarrow$ supporting the staff in TQM implementation

• Builds a positive connection between that committee and the traditional supervisors in the school and/or district

b. Use advice from consultants and/or from schools that have succeeded at TQM transformation.

The latter action is particularly important. People who have learned things the hard way can save you much time and trouble with practical advice on such things as the importance of developing teaming skills, the value of limiting the number of major improvement task forces operating at one time, and the need to select improvement priorities carefully.

Figure 47

TQM

Special Considerations

1. Using research to improve teaching and learning
2. Making learning a pleasant experience
3. Using technology
4. Using checklists

D. Special Considerations

This guide presents only the framework for a currently validated system for teaching. Research in the cognitive and neuroscience areas is continuing at a rapid pace. Therefore, the first suggestion under closing special considerations in Figure 47 is that every educator must be a student who keeps learning about new discoveries, models, and improved practices in teaching. Fortunately, there are some concerned and talented people working for organizations and publishers who focus on making the latest information available to teachers and administrators. The final section in this guide directs you to resources that will help keep you current in the field.

The second consideration listed in Figure 47 is a reminder on a very well researched point that could get lost among the many system details in this guide. That point is that students are encouraged to work at learning if the experience provides enjoyment and, yes, even fun. Students, like all of us, tend to be attracted to pleasant experiences. For that reason, sources for materials that make learning unique and enjoyable are included in the resource section.

Third, the world of technology has created new resources that can help teachers and trainers provide variety in tasks and learning style opportunities. More interactive programs are replacing textbook-on-the-screen types of software. Our reference lists encourage you to select software to pursue the model of brain-compatible learning and to make the analysis of data easier.

Finally, we provide some simple checklists that will aid you in planning an effective teaching system. Figure 48 on page 112 provides a page-numbered listing of resources in Section E. The checklists in this last section can help you to summarize and apply the action suggestions from the guide. Meanwhile, please keep this major theme in mind:

Quality
is a
direction!

W. Edwards Deming said it another way: "It is not instant pudding!" Administrators should concentrate on encouraging and supporting, not on announcing and mandating. The checklists in Section E have been constructed in a supporting context.

Figure 48

TQM Listing of Resources
The System Secret to Quality Teaching and Learning

E. Teacher and Administrator Checklists and Resources

Here is a guide to the listing of resources provided in Figure 48:

Administrator Checklist on Supporting the Use of a Brain-Compatible Teaching System. Administrators need to know about, stay informed on, inform others on, and support teachers in this area.

Teacher Checklist on Using a Brain-Compatible Teaching System. Teachers need to practice the fundamental techniques and keep abreast of new research.

Special Learning Survey. Once you teach brain-compatible principles to your students, use this as an alternative to the student questionnaire on pages 84 and 85 if you wish. Or, use it as the basis for oral questions to younger students.

Using Longer Time Blocks Effectively in Classrooms and Labs. Be careful about lengthened periods. Be sure you do it in a brain-compatible way.

Multimedia and Multiple Intelligences. Use this checklist to think about ways to amplify your ability to provide different learning options to students with different talents.

Administrator Checklist on Supporting Total Quality Management. Knowing about, encouraging, and supporting TQM are the keys to growing a culture of continuous improvement.

Teacher Checklist on Using Total Quality Management. The classroom and student-teacher partnerships are the front line of continuous improvement in learning. A teacher and class can evaluate their progress together in this area.

Books, Videos, and "Stuff." A few specific books are listed. However, the major focus is on sources of new books and information in the field.

Software and Web Sites. Beyond the multimedia checklist, be sure to check on software and Web sites for new information.

These resources help emphasize two major points about this guide on a teaching system:

1. *The guide is dedicated to the management of effective instruction, not to the "management" of students.* It is certainly true that relevant, compatible, individualized instruction is a major component of a productive class environment. Nonetheless, the direct focus of this guide is on effective learning, not on "good discipline" in the classroom.

2. *The proper use of data analysis is a fundamental component of quality management.* This is as true in managing effective instruction and learning as it is in any other field. It is true whether or not one is a fan of the No Child Left Behind Act.

The resources on the following pages will provide any educator with practical guidance on pursuing these two areas: effective instruction and proper use of data analysis.

Administrator Checklist on Supporting the Use of a Brain-Compatible Teaching System

Answer
"Yes" or **"No"**

_____ 1. I have attended one or more awareness seminars on brain-compatible teaching and have a plan to keep informed in this developing area. The plan is:

_____

_____

_____

_____ 2. I have arranged awareness and/or professional development seminars on brain-compatible techniques for staff members, school board members, and parents. New staff members are oriented in this area.

_____ 3. I have supported the acquisition of media and library materials on brain-compatible teaching and learning.

_____ 4. I have supported the creation and operation of a staff task force to promote brain-compatible teaching on a continuous improvement basis.

_____ 5. Our school (district) has initiated free and convenient parent-awareness programs on brain-compatible learning and growing intelligence.

_____ 6. Our school (district) exchanges information with other schools (districts) in the area of brain-compatible teaching and learning. Staff representatives attend conferences and expositions and bring information back to others.

_____ 7. Our school (district) curricula provide students with an awareness of brain models and skills in using them.

_____ 8. Our staff and students use statistical measurements and portfolios to document, celebrate, and improve different forms of learning.

_____ 9. Our helping evaluation program includes standards on the use of brain-compatible teaching principles.

_____ 10. Student success and career planning include attention to different learning styles and talents.

Name _____ **Title** _____ **Date** _____

Teacher Checklist on Using a Brain-Compatible Teaching System

DIRECTIONS: This checklist can be used by an individual or a team for self-evaluation and self-direction on continuous improvement or as a guide for a portion of a formal evaluation review supporting continuous progress (*not* an "I-gotcha" evaluation with some expectation of rapid perfection).

_____
(Yes or No)

1. I (we) have completed one or more formal courses or seminars on brain-compatible teaching. List: _____

_____

2. I (we) have a plan to continue gaining knowledge and skills in this evolving area. Example(s): _____

_____

3. I (we) use a lesson planning approach designed to promote the use of brain-compatible principles. Describe: _____

_____

4. My (our) course and units currently include the elements as marked:

Element	Check one column for each element.			
	All units	**Some units**	**I've started**	**None**
a. Anchoring/Motivation				
b. A connection or "hook"				
c. Pre-assessment				
d. A sequence of learning → doing → reflecting				
e. Learning style options				
f. Processing or talent options				
g. Use of visual organizers				
h. Observance of the Beginning-End-Middle (BEM) principle with pulse learning				
i. Use of a mastery process				
j. Specific activities focused on cooperative learning and the development of emotional intelligence				
k. Documentation and celebration				
l. Helping students learn and apply the brain-compatible and continuous improvement principles				

_____

5. I (we) work with a formal team of peers to increase our use of brain-compatible and continuous improvement techniques. Describe:

_____

Name _____, **Date** _____, **Check one: Self** _____
With others _____

Subject _____   **Teacher** _____

Date _____   **Special Learning Survey** _____

DIRECTIONS: Check *one* column for each question.

	Answer		
	A **Always,** **or Yes**	**B** **Usually**	**C** **Never,** **or No**
1. I feel welcome and safe in this class. (A, B, or C)			
2. The teacher shows us how the subject matter is important in the real world. (A, B, or C)			
3. We spend the right amount of time (not too long, not too short) on individual activities. (A, B, or C)			
4. When I have trouble learning one way, the teacher gives me a different way to learn. (A, B, or C)			
5. I know which way I learn best (auditory, visual, hands-on or doing, alone, or on a team). (A or C)			
6. The teacher allows different students to show that they have learned in different ways. (A, B, or C)			
7. I know *my* best talent (linguistic, logic or math, visual, kinesthetic, interpersonal, intrapersonal) for working on most problems. (A or C)			
8. The teacher helps us use lots of visual organizers. (A, B, or C)			
9. When I need special help, the teacher provides it. (A, B, or C)			
10. I am continuously improving my knowledge in this class. (A or C)			

Using Longer Time Blocks Effectively in Classrooms and Labs

Teacher Guide

Longer time blocks can increase or decrease the efficiency of student learning. Consider these potential impacts of longer periods:

Possible Positive Effects	Possible Negative Effects
Allows more focus on real-life complex tasks or projects. This gives more meaning to learning activities.	Greatly lowers learning if a teacher uses primarily one type of learning activity (especially lecturing) for most of the period.
Provides more opportunity for cooperative or team-based learning activities that develop important interpersonal and partnership skills.	Greatly lowers learning if a teacher fails to observe anchoring and affirmation principles. More time in a tense situation harms learning.
Allows time for different kinds of learning activities useful to students who learn in different ways or with different talents or "intelligences."	Leads to less learning and more wasting of time if the period is not planned thoroughly in advance.
Gives a teacher an opportunity to get to know each student better and to work with each individual to encourage mastery.	Is confusing to students if too many items of information (excess chunking) are incorporated in one time block.

Here are several important principles from brain or learning research that can help any teacher gain the positive effects and avoid the negative effects from longer time blocks:

1. *Anchoring.* When learning is approached in longer doses, it is more important than ever to begin a course with anchoring activities. These are activities designed to make each student feel welcome ("I'm glad *you* are here"), interested in the course ("I'm going to give you some new power"), and confident ("You will be able to succeed here"). One of the best ways to ensure anchoring is to use brainstorming in a department or teaching team to equip each teacher with a list of possible anchoring activities. Then each teacher should plan and implement those particular activities with which he or she is most comfortable.

2. *Pulsed learning.* Research shows that the most learning occurs at the beginning and end of new activities. Long middles are a mistake. So follow the BEM (beginning-end-middle) principle by using pulsed learning:

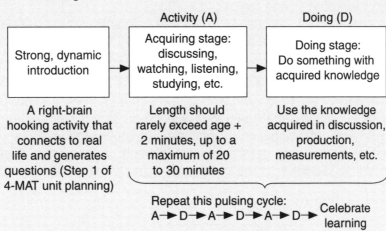

If you have not been trained in pulsed learning, be sure to seek such training. The pulsed approach is critical to avoid the boredom ("brain shutdown") that occurs if a long period is used to import an excessive amount of information to students without the opportunity to change activities or use the information. The chunking principle can be observed here too—Avoid presenting more than seven pieces of information at one time.

3. *Complex, real-life tasks.* "Doing," or using information and various skills, will bring about much more long-term learning, especially if the tasks resemble those that students might encounter in the workplace someday. The complex outcomes approach to learning works better than excessive emphasis on discrete objectives:

Photography Course Example

Objective   Complex task

Objective	Complex task
Take a "good" picture (*good* as defined by a list of standards)	Take four to six "good" pictures and compose a clear photographic essay for the school newspaper on a topic approved in advance by the teacher

4. *Cooperative learning or teaming.* When students work together in teams, they can learn the interpersonal skills that are useful in most careers. Many students will be energized by the opportunity to work with others. This is especially true for those who have a high preference for using interpersonal talent or "intelligence," but all students should develop talent in this area. Of course, teachers must plan the opportunities for teamwork carefully. Longer periods make teamwork much more feasible.

5. *A mastery focus.* Having the time for team teaching makes mastery learning possible:

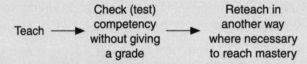

Teach ⟶ Check (test) competency without giving a grade ⟶ Reteach in another way where necessary to reach mastery

Student peers can assist in reteaching activities, while other students who have mastered material go on to enrichment or advanced (beyond required) learning. The "how" of reteaching should focus on learning styles or learning options.

6. *Learning options.* Longer periods make it easier to arrange different ways of learning so that a student having difficulty can be given an opportunity to learn in the way he or she learns best. Planning of visual, auditory, kinesthetic, and interpersonal learning options and/or of options on ways to demonstrate learning give a course two powers:
   a. The power of giving a student maximum learning help by having available his or her preferred way of learning
   b. The power of having enrichment activities that help students increase their talent in a particular multiple intelligence area

Many computer programs are now available to support the use of these powers. See the "Multimedia and Multiple Intelligences" resource sheet on page 119.

7. *Total Quality Management.* In longer periods, a teacher can get to know each student better. This provides an improved opportunity to give each student more help and guidance on continuous improvement in the personal development of knowledge, skills, and habits. One of the best gifts to each student is to get the student focused on the goal of "better"—"This work is better than what I did last time; let me place it in my portfolio and record it on my personal data chart."

Multimedia and Multiple Intelligences

Figure 16 on page 32 shows multiple intelligences grouped in the four quadrants of a preference test. Here, we surround that quadrant chart with relevant types of computer programs:

Abstract thinking

• Writing and listening experiences • Spreadsheets, calculations, analysis	• Linguistic • Logical-mathematical	• Visual • Musical	• Drawing and organizing patterns • Composing
• Simulations for individual decision making • Nature experiences on screen	• Intrapersonal • Naturalist	• Kinesthetic • Interpersonal	• Move-and-construct software • Group interaction, including Internet activities

Experience-based thinking

Some software firms, like Tom Snyder Productions, specialize in constructing multimedia programs that are interactive and multisensory and that encourage critical thinking or concrete action. In addition, many learning segments and tasks are now available on the Internet for preschool through K–12 and college levels.

When you evaluate software or Internet activities, consider the following checklist. The more "yes" responses you can give, the more appropriate the selection:

"Yes" or "No"

_____ 1. The selection involves tasks and/or learning styles (see, hear, do) appropriate for the student(s).

_____ 2. You have previewed the selection and prepared specific objectives and directions for use, perhaps including visual organizers.

_____ 3. The selection promotes action or interactivity to solidify learning.

_____ 4. The selection offers a real-life context that the student(s) can appreciate.

_____ 5. The selection is appropriate for the performance level of the student(s)—reading and/or vocabulary level and background.

_____ 6. The selection and your use plan allow related communication activities to occur among students.

_____ 7. The selection and your use plan provide choices for the student(s).

Administrator Checklist on Supporting Total Quality Management

Answer
"Yes" or **"No"**

_____   1. I have attended one or more awareness seminars on total quality management and I have a plan to keep informed in this area. The plan is:

_____

_____

_____

_____   2. My school board and the entire staff have been presented with an awareness seminar on the basic principles of quality management, including the concept of continuous improvement in pursuing defined missions, the need for a system approach based on models of operation, attention to human needs, and the importance of using data properly to manage improvement efforts.

_____   3. The school board has voted in favor of a specific policy supporting the use of quality management principles in our district or school.

_____   4. I have supported the acquisition of media and library materials on quality management and quality tools in education.

_____   5. Staff members have been given specific training on the expectations and use of quality management tools in the district, school, and classroom.

_____   6. The school or district provides parents and students with information on the quality process.

_____   7. The school and/or district supports proper data gathering and analysis to make the processes as simple and convenient as possible for teachers and students.

_____   8. One or more staff task forces gives direction to our quality efforts, coordinating them with the state testing program and other school procedures.

_____   9. An integrated quality curriculum for students has been implemented, one that uses portfolios and measurement to prepare students for quality procedures in business and industry.

_____   10. Our staff orientation and helping evaluation programs give specific attention to the use of quality management procedures in the classroom.

Name _____   **Title** _____   **Date** _____

Teacher Checklist on Using Total Quality Management

DIRECTIONS: This checklist can be used by an individual or a team for self-evaluation and self-direction on quality management processes in the classroom.

_____ 1. I (we) have completed one or more formal courses or seminars on quality
(Yes or No)   management learning. List: _____

_____ 2. I (we) have a plan for continuing to gain knowledge and skills in this area.
           Example(s): _____

_____ 3. My (our) course and units currently include the elements as marked:

Element	Check one column for each element.			
	All units	**Some units**	**I've started**	**None**
a. Clear course and unit mission objectives				
b. Use of pre-assessment data				
c. Learning options for students				
d. Self-evaluation options for students (example: rubrics)				
e. Formative assessment and mastery options				
f. Careful use of achievement data and factor relationships to guide improvement efforts				
g. Application of quality management principles by students				
h. Documentation and celebration of learning				

_____ 4. I (we) work with a formal team of peers to increase my (our) use of quality
           management techniques for improving student achievement.

Name _____ Date _____ Check one: Self _____
                                                         With others _____

Books, Videos, and "Stuff"

Sources for Materials on Brain-Compatible Teaching

The Brain Store. This San Diego source established by Eric Jensen offers the most complete source of K–12 materials, excellent books by Eric Jensen and others, videos, and software. The store can supply a printed catalog and information on outstanding seminars and Brain Expos around the nation. http://www.thebrainstore.com/store/. 1-800-325-4769.

Kagan Publishing & Professional Development. Kagan's catalog is especially strong on multiple intelligences and cooperative learning. A series of "Smart Cards" is available that offers excellent summaries on brain-based teaching. 1-800-933-2667.

Trainer's Warehouse. This company provides tools, tips, and toys for teaching. Gadgets, puzzle software, and certificates can all add pizzazz and fun to classes. http://www.trainerswarehouse.com. 1-800-299-3770.

Zephyr Press. This K–12 source is located in Tucson, Arizona. The useful Zephyr catalog is available in print or on the Web at http://www.zephyrpress.com. 1-800-232-2187.

Sources for Materials on Quality Management in Education

American Society for Quality (ASQ). Go to ASQ's Web site. On the left sidebar, click on *Books and Publications* and then "Education Library" under *Areas of Use*. The Bookstore page has a *Browse Bookstore* feature; select "Education" from the drop-down menu. All available education titles are now listed; any title can be selected to get information and to purchase.

Koalaty Kid. ASQ also operates a K–12 quality education initiative. To learn about members (more than 200 schools and organizations), conferences, and training programs, go to http://www.asq.org/edu/kkid/whatis.html. You may also call 1-800-248-1946 for information on training sessions.

Sources for Materials on Staff Development

Association for Supervision and Curriculum Development (ASCD). This large and respected professional organization, headquartered in Alexandria, Virginia, provides all types of publications and professional development materials, including books and videos on brain-based instruction and on quality schools by outstanding experts. The association also sponsors large annual conferences on instructional improvement. http://www.ascd.org. 1-800-933-2723.

Corwin Press. This company specializes in publishing professional development materials for teachers and administrators. In addition, many of its distinguished authors are available as speakers. Their books cover such topics as differentiated instruction, thinking maps, mastery teaching, data-driven differentiation, brain processes, whole-brain leadership, and collaborative (empowering) leadership. http://www.corwinpress.com. 1-800-818-7243.

Video Journal of Education and Teachstream. This company produces new staff-development videos annually. Their series has included excellent presentations on both brain-based learning and the quality school movement. http://www.teachstream.com. 1-800-572-1153.

Specific Books That Can Be Very Useful

1. *The Accelerated Learning Handbook* by Dave Meier (New York: McGraw Hill, 2000). This book is also very useful for industry trainers. It focuses on different learning styles.
2. *Brain-Based Learning* by Eric Jensen (San Diego: The Brain Store, 2000). Available from the Brain Store (under "Sources for Materials on Brain-Compaitable Teaching"). This is just one of *many* outstanding books by Eric Jensen, one of the most prolific writers and popular workshop leaders in the field of brain-compatible teaching. Also consider two

of his other books: *Different Brains, Different Learners* (San Diego: The Brain Store, 2000), on helping hard-to-reach learners, and *Tools for Engagement: Managing Emotional States for Learner Success* (San Diego: The Brain Store, 2003), on research-tested techniques to enhance learning states.

3. *Discover Your Child's Learning Style* by Mariaemma Willis and Victoria Kindle-Hodson (Roseville, CA: Prima Publishing, 1999). This paperback is a best buy for both parents and teachers who want a thorough and practical review of how to identify and work with students' different learning styles.

4. *Excel Charts* by John Walkenbach (New York: John Wiley & Sons, 2003). This 516-page volume goes far beyond what most classroom teachers need to learn. However, it could be useful for data or computer specialists at the school or district level in covering advanced charting and statistical analysis techniques.

5. *Future Force* by Elaine McClanchan and Carolyn Wicks (Chino Hills, CA: Pact Publishing, 1999. Available from ASQ Quality Press). This is one of the best books on useful activities for teaching quality principles in K–12 classrooms. It can help you teach quality in brain-compatible ways.

6. *How to Give It So They Get It* by Sharon Bowman (Glenbrook, NV: Bowperson Publishing, 1998). This delightful 225-page paperback provides a practical approach to learning styles and a powerful brain-compatible lesson plan format called the "Flight Plan." All of Sharon Bowman's books can be very useful to any teacher. They are available at http://www.amazon.com. Consider *Shake Rattle & Roll* (Glenbrook, NV: Bowperson Publishing, 1999) for really fun classroom activities. Also consider *Preventing Death by Lecture* (Glenbrook, NV: Bowperson Publishing, 2001) and *Presenting with Pizzazz* (Glenbrook, NV: Bowperson Publishing, 1997).

7. *How to Meet Standards, Motivate Students, and Still Enjoy Teaching* by Barbara P. Benson (Thousand Oaks, CA: Corwin Press, 2003). This book provides direction for K–12 classrooms in pursuing four practices that improve learning while teaching to state and national standards. Brain-compatible techniques are emphasized.

8. *Improving Student Learning: Applying Deming's Quality Principles in the Classroom,* 2nd Ed., by Lee Jenkins (Milwaukee, WI: ASQ Quality Press, 2003). First published in 1996, this new edition gives specific examples of how to measure improvement. Lee Jenkins successfully led his school district in the use of Deming's quality principles and is now a consultant to many other districts. His examples are based on actual classroom information. This is one of the many ASQ education library books (see contact information on page 122).

9. *The Learning Revolution* by Gordon Dryden and Dr. Jeannette Vos (Torrance, CA: The Learning Web, 1999). This is one of the best books for school board members and administrators to gain a global perspective on what is truly a revolution in brain-compatible learning. Consider visiting the Web site at http://www.thelearningweb.net.

10. *Let Me Learn* by Christine A. Johnston (Thousand Oaks, CA: Corwin Press, 1998). This book on different learning styles has a powerful message that comes from descriptions of learning experiences from different students. Proponents of narrow word- and number-based assessment tests and related absolute written test scores should all be "sentenced" to reading this book.

11. *Microsoft Office Excel 2003 Quick Steps* by John Cronan (Emeryville, CA: McGraw-Hill/Osborne, 2004). This 206-page, softcover, colorful, *visual* how-to manual is one good example of the type of practical learning resource that can help teachers use a computer effectively. The charting and data analysis sections provide a foundation for the use of Excel, an important tool for educators. Visit http://www.osborne.com for publisher information.

12. *Multiple Intelligences in the Classroom* by Thomas Armstrong (Alexandria, VA: Association for Supervision and Curriculum Development, 2000; contact information provided on page 122). This is one of the most practical and current reviews of the multiple intelligences model.

13. *The New Philosophy for K–12 Education: A Deming Framework for Transforming America's Schools* by James F. Leonard (Milwaukee, WI: ASQ Quality Press, 1996; contact information on page 122). This hardcover book provides a scholarly and practical bridge from the work of Deming to application in schools. The author is an engineer, college teacher, past student of Deming, school board member, and consultant to both schools and industry. His presentations led the staff of Minuteman Regional High School (used as an example in this guide) to a state of enthusiasm for total quality management in the classroom.

14. *Right-Brained Children in a Left-Brained World* by Jeffrey Freed and Laurie Parsons (New York: Simon and Schuster, 1997). This is a book that every educator and parent should read. It helps anyone to understand brains that have been "wired" differently by our multimedia environment. Too often, students who learn differently become the victims of labels rather than the beneficiaries of teaching techniques adjusted to the way they learn best.

15. *The Small Business Guerrilla Guide to Six Sigma* by Jay Arthur (Denver, CO: LifeStar Publishing, 2004). This book is a useful way for a teacher, administrator, or school board member to learn about quality philosophy and procedures in business as we prepare students for that world. It was produced by the author of QI Macros for Excel, software recommended later in this section.

16. *Statistics Made Simple for School Leaders* by Susan Rovezzi Carroll and David J. Carroll (Lanham, MD: Scarecrow Press, 2002). This paperback was produced in cooperation with the American Association of School Administrators. It is a primer on data-driven decision making and communication, with one of the best overviews on statistics for educators.

17. *Thinking Tools for Kids: An Activity Book for Classroom Learning* by Barbara A. Cleary and Sally J. Duncan (Milwaukee, WI: ASQ Quality Press, 1999). This book focuses on the use of quality tools by elementary school students. Brainstorming, fishbone (cause-and-effect) diagrams, bar charts, line graphs, Pareto charts—they are all applied in the elementary classroom with a home connection. This 166-page paperback is a superior resource that secondary school teachers could also use effectively.

Software and Web Sites

Gradebook Programs

Here, the recommendation is that you do research and look at different programs. A Google search on "gradebook programs" will yield more than 62,000 hits. Look at some of the sites on the first few pages. Check advertisements in professional magazines and educational software catalogs. Products appear and disappear regularly. Talk with teachers in schools using gradebook software. Consider these factors:

- Ease of use
- Platform compatibility (Macintosh and Windows)
- Ability to transfer data to and from your school's student information system
- Types of data analysis, charts, and reports provided (are they what you want?)

Here are two different programs used at Minuteman Regional High School:

- Bobbing GradeBook for Macintosh. Visit their Web site at http://www.bobbingsoftware.com. It produced the figures on pages 4 and 72 of this guide.
- GradeQuick 8 for Windows and Macintosh. Visit their Web site at http://www.jacksoncorp.com.

Spreadsheets and Charting

- *Microsoft Excel.* This program can take spreadsheet data and create such charts as column, bar, line, pie, scatter, and stacked. It can calculate average and sum and produce a trend line. With an add-in toolpack, it can calculate mean, standard error, median, mode, standard deviation, correlation, and other advanced statistics.
- *QI Macros for Excel.* This subprogram installs in Excel for Macintosh or Windows. It makes production of basic charts *very easy*, including line, run, bar or column, pie, Pareto, scatter, and histograms. It can even produce control charts. It also works with the statistical analysis tools mentioned in the description of Excel. The program is inexpensive ($129 or less in quantity). QI Macros for Excel is available from:

  LifeStar
  2244 South Olive Street
  Denver, Colorado 80224-2518
  Fax 1-888-468-1536
  Orders: 1-888-468-1535
  Questions: 1-888-468-1537
  Web site: http://www.qimacros.com

By combining Excel and QI Macros for Excel, a school or district can create its own customized data analysis programs. Charts made in Excel can be transferred to Microsoft PowerPoint for display purposes.

State Test Data

Many states offer downloadable data summary tables on state test results. For example, in Massachusetts, the state hired dataMetrics Software to prepare data tables at no cost to school districts. Schools can download this data in various report forms in a program called TestWiz:Massachusetts, a Windows-based product. Minuteman Regional High School uses some of these reports as is and transfers other data into Excel with QI Macros for production of analytic charts. Consult your State Department of Education for test data that it can provide.

Rubrics

Rubrics are an important evaluation tool and data source. Here are two sources of help in this area:

- *RubiStar.* Visit http://rubistar.4teachers.org/index.php. RubiStar is a *free* tool for helping teachers make rubrics.
- *Ten Sigma.* This company in Mankato, Minnesota, supplies software for easy construction of rubrics and K–12 collections of rubrics in most subjects. http://www.tensigma.org. 1-800-657-3815.

Useful Student Programs

Secondary-level students can and should use Excel, PowerPoint, and other programs that are common in the workplace. However, quality activities on the elementary level are best supported by more basic programs. Tom Snyder Productions, a Scholastic Company (http://www.tomsnyder.com; 1-800-342-0236), provides these excellent programs for use in elementary schools:

Program	Grades and Function	Excellent for . . .
Graph Club 2.0 (Mac/Win)	K–4 Graphs and analysis	• Picture, bar, circle, and line graphs and tables • Rubric assessments
Graph Master (Mac/Win)	4–8 Graphs and analysis	• Bar, pictograph, circle, line, scatter, frequency, histogram, line plot, and box plot graphs • Calculating mean, median, mode, and more
Scholastic Keys (Win), for use with Microsoft Office	K–5 Lower-level equivalents of Microsoft Word, Excel, and PowerPoint	• Spreadsheets • Charts and graphs • Presentations • Flyers, letters, etc.

Be sure to consult the source addresses or Web sites for listed materials because availability can change and improved products become available over time.

Comprehensive Process Control

For districts ready to move into a *comprehensive* quality management program, consider PathMaker. This relatively inexpensive but powerful Windows program provides project pathways and decision-making tools and includes full data-analysis and charting capabilities through control charts. For more information contact:

SkyMark
7300 Penn Avenue
Pittsburgh, PA 15208
1-800-826-7284
http://www.skymark.com

Glossary

Some terms are used differently in this book than in some other books. This brief glossary clarifies some important words or terms. It can also be useful for review purposes.

anchoring—Saying and doing things that help your students feel comfortable and safe in your classroom.

brain research—Investigations into how the brain reacts or works. The research is not limited to one source field, such as neuroscience, cognitive experimentation, or observations. In education, practical information comes from all of these sources.

cause-and-effect diagram—A chart identifying factors that are judged important in contributing to a result. The generic construction is:

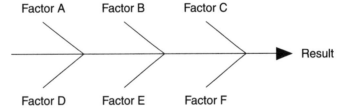

The factors can be placed in a numbered sequence or process, but that is optional. So, do not assume that every cause-and-effect diagram is also a process chart.

charts—Visual summaries of data that facilitate the analysis and use of the data. See the discussion of different chart types, beginning on page 77.

correlation—A numerical measurement of the relationship between two factors where:

+1 = a direct relationship (when one factor increases, the other increases)

0 = no direct relationship

–1 = a reverse relationship (when one factor increases, the other decreases)

hook—Providing students with a unique experience or connection that shows them the real-life relevance of the subject and stimulates their curiosity about it.

learning style—A way of perceiving or receiving information. For example, many students prefer to get information in a visual rather than an auditory format.

mastery teaching—A process in which not-for-grade testing is used to determine whether learning has taken place, and reteaching is pursued where learning has not yet been achieved.

mean—The average of a set or series of scores.

median—The middle score in a set or series of scores.

mode—The most frequent score in a set or series of scores.

PDCA—This acronym stands for a sequence of Plan → Do → Check → Act/Adjust. In this book, it refers to:

1. Planning your curriculum and teaching techniques
2. Doing the teaching
3. Checking the results with measurement tools
4. Adjusting continued and/or future teaching materials and techniques to gain improved results

In the world of teaching, the word *adjust* is a more specific description than the word *act* as used in many business textbooks.

preference test—A set of questions that helps a student know more about himself or herself. For example, a brain preference test can help a student be aware of his or her preferred styles of learning or thinking.

process—A sequence of steps or activities designed to achieve some result. For example, a Plan → Do → Check → Act/Adjust process is recommended in this book as a sequence for guiding the use of recommended teaching techniques from the SMART TEACHING system.

rubrics—Published performance standards, often in checklist form, for evaluating specific types of projects or assignments. These can be very useful for students in evaluating their own work as well as for analyzing what standards need adjusted teaching attention.

standard deviation—A calculation of the degree of spread in a set of scores. When seeking improvement, you are often attempting to lower the deviation spread so that more grades are closer to the higher, desirable end of the grade spectrum.

system or subsystem—A related group of elements or factors, such as a set of teaching techniques for improving student learning. Since the word *system* is so often used to refer to everything about a school district ("the X school system"), note that the word is really referring to a subsystem in this book. The book presents a system of teaching techniques labeled SMART TEACHING.

talent—A way of processing information or solving problems. Also called an *intelligence* or a *thinking style*. The theory of multiple intelligences advanced by Dr. Howard Gardner defines a set of different talents or thinking styles.

TQM—An acronym for *total quality management* with the words having this meaning in this book:

Total—to be used in *all* classrooms, not sporadically or just in some classes

Quality—the pursuit of continuous improvement

Management—the use of models and measurement data to adjust processes in order to pursue improvement

Some textbooks now use the acronym TQE to stand for *total quality education* in schools.

Index